CONVEYANCING
Contents

Introduction

INTRODUCTION

This book is not a substitute for a qualified professional and is not presented as such. The information contained within is for use as guidance and at all times the advice of professionals should be sought, as only the extremely confident and experienced lay person, or actual practitioner can buy or sell property alone.

Usually, when buying or selling residential property, solicitors or licensed conveyancers are normally used in order to ensure that the transaction proceeds smoothly. However, the actual processes of conveyancing are usually a mystery to both buyer and seller who are not privy to the procedures.

The aim of this brief but concise book is to throw some light on the *basic* processes, thus ensuring that those who are involved at least have some understanding of what is happening and can question those acting for them at any given point. The book should be read in conjunction with " A Straightforward Guide to Buying and Selling Property" which deals with the more general aspects such as the involvement of estate agents.

This new edition includes information about the 2002 Land Registration Act, which came into effect in 2003. Also, recent seller's information forms, introduced to enhance pre-contract enquiries usually carried out by solicitors are included. The government has carried out work on the principles and practice of the seller's information pack, which they are trying to introduce into law. This requires all sellers to provide as much information as is possible about their properties, to the purchaser, in order to ensure an open sales process and a possible speedier move towards completion of sale.

At the moment, a pilot is being carried out in relation to a seller's property survey. This particular, contentious, part of the legislation will require all sellers to carry out a structural survey of their property before offering it for sale. This will probably take some time to come into force, if at all in its current proposed form. However, as a start, the government has introduced seller's information forms that they are encouraging all solicitors to send to sellers, requiring them to provide detailed information about their property.

Although it is safe to say that the average basic conveyance of a leasehold flat or freehold house is relatively simple and unproblematic, there are still fundamental ground rules, which one must observe.

When purchasing a leasehold flat for example, particularly in a multi-occupied block, the lease has to be very closely scrutinised and all the covenants in the lease understood. Leases can be unintelligible documents, couched in redundant language, badly laid out and misleading at the best of times.

Leases contain landlord and tenants covenants, which impose rights and obligations on the respective parties, particularly in relation to repairing obligations and service charge and ground rent payments. Other covenants may impose an onerous burden on the leaseholder and quite often only an experienced eye can pick this up.

Likewise, the freehold transfer document may contain obligations, which can only be picked up or understood, by an experienced eye.

Therefore, even if you decide to carry out conveyancing yourself you should always get a sound second opinion concerning the lease or freehold document.

In addition, as we will see later, there are two forms of conveyancing in existence, *registered* and *unregistered*. The former means that the ownership of land and all that entails, including extent of ownership, is registered at the Land Registry. The very fact of registration ensures that legal title can be verified. Unregistered land has to be proven through production of deeds, which can be time consuming and problematic. Land Registration has been compulsory in the United Kingdom for a while now, but it is still a fact that over 30% of all property is unregistered.

This book details the processes of conveyancing as it affects both registered and unregistered land. It then goes on to deal with the advanced stages of conveyancing as it affects unregistered land and also the process of conveying registered land.

Following the conclusion, there is a glossary of terms and a list of useful addresses. There is an appendix, which outlines Land Registry forms currently in use for conveyancing property..

Finally this book cannot guarantee that you will be in a position to convey property without expert help, precisely because it is a guide to conveyancing. However, it should enlighten you as to the processes.

1

LIBRARY & INFORMATION

CONVEYANCING IN CONTEXT

Conveyancing, or the practice of conveyancing, is about how to transfer the ownership of land and property from one person or organisation to another. Land and property can include freehold property, leasehold property (residential) or can include business leases.

It is principally the conveyance of residential property that this book is concerned with.

Essentially, the process of conveyancing lays down clear procedures for the conveyancer and also sets out each party's position during the sale or acquisition.

Before understanding the process of conveyancing, however, it is essential to understand something about the legal forms of ownership of property.

Legal ownership of property

There are two main forms of legal ownership of property in England and Wales If you are about to embark on the sale or acquisition of a house or flat (or business) then you will be dealing in the main with either freehold or leasehold property.

It is very rare indeed to find other forms of ownership, although, with the advent of the Commonhold and Leasehold Reform Act 2002, which became law in May 2002, the government has introduced a form of ownership called 'common hold' that will, in essence, create the freehold ownership of flats, with common responsibility for communal areas. As the Act is new, and is being introduced in phases, it will be a while before the first Commonhold properties are created.

Freehold property

In general, if you own the freehold of a house or a piece of land, then you will be the outright owner with no fixed period of time and no one else to answer to (with the exception of statutory authorities).

There may be registered restrictions on title, which we will be discussing later. The property will probably be subject to a mortgage so the only other overriding interest will be that of the bank or the building society. The responsibility for repairs and maintenance and general upkeep will be the freeholders. The law can intervene if certain standards are not maintained.

The deed to your house will be known as the "freehold transfer document" which will contain any rights and obligations. Usually, the transfer document will list any "encumbrances" (restrictions) on the use of the land, such as rights of way of other parties, sales restrictions etc.

The deeds to your home are the most important documentation. As we will see later, without deeds and historical data, such as the root of title, it can be rather complicated selling property. This is why the system of land registration in use in this country has greatly simplified property transactions.

Any person owning freehold property is free to create another interest in land, such as a lease or a weekly or monthly tenancy, subject to any restrictions the transfer may contain.

Leasehold property

If a person lives in a property owned by someone else and has an agreement for a period of time, usually a long period, over 21 years and up to 99 years or 125 years, in some cases 999 years, then they are a leaseholder. The conveyancing of leasehold property is, potentially, far more problematic than freehold property, particularly when the flat is in a block with a number of units.

The lease is a contract between landlord and tenant which lays down the rights and obligations of both parties and should be read thoroughly by both the leaseholder and, in particular, the conveyancer. Once signed then the purchaser is bound by all the clauses in the contract.

It is worth looking at the nature of a lease before discussing the rather more complex process of conveyancing. Again, it has to be stated that it is of the utmost importance that both the purchaser and the vendor understand the nature of a lease.

The lease

Preamble

The start of a lease is called the preamble. This defines the landlord and purchaser and also the nature of the property in question (the demise). It will also detail the remaining period of the lease.

Leaseholders covenants

Covenants are best understood as obligations and responsibilities. Leaseholder's covenants are therefore a list of things that leaseholders should do, such as pay their service charges and keep the interior of the dwelling in good repair and not, for example, to alter the structure. The landlord's covenants will set out the obligations of the landlord, which is usually to maintain the structure and exterior of the block, light common parts etc.

One unifying theme of all leasehold property is that, notwithstanding the landlord's responsibilities, it is the leaseholder who will pay for everything out of a service charge.

Leases will make detailed provisions for the setting, managing and charging of service charges, which should include a section on accounting. All landlords of leaseholders are accountable under the Landlord and Tenant Act 1985, as amended by the 1987 Act. These Acts will regulate the way a landlord treats a leaseholder in the charging and accounting of service charges.

In addition, the 1996 Housing Act and the Commonhold and Leasehold Reform Act 2002 has provided further legislation protecting leaseholders by introducing the right of leaseholders to go to Leasehold Valuation Tribunals if they are unhappy with levels and management of charges and also to carry out audits of charges.

It is vital when buying a leasehold property that you read the lease. Leases tend to be different from each other and nothing can be assumed. When you buy a property, ensure that the person selling has paid all debts and has contributed to some form of "sinking fund" whereby provision has been built up for major repairs in the future. Make sure that you will not be landed with big bills after moving in and that, if you are, there is money to deal with them. After a lease has been signed then there is little or no recourse to recoup any money owed.

These are all the finer points of leases and the conveyancer has to be very vigilant. In particular read the schedules to the lease as these sometimes contain rather more detail.

One of the main differences between leasehold and freehold property is that the lease is a long tenancy agreement which contains provisions which give the landlord rather a lot of power to manage (or mismanage) and it is always a possibility that a leaseholder can be forced to give up his or her home in the event of non-compliance with the terms of the lease. This is known as forfeiture.

Under the Commonhold and Leasehold Reform Act 2002 referred to earlier, a new 'no fault right to manage' has been introduced. This will enable leaseholders who are unhappy with the management of their property, to take over the management with relative ease. The Act will apply to most landlords, with the exception of Local Authorities.

These new powers will go a long way to curb the excesses or inefficiencies of numerous landlords and will provide more control and greater security for leaseholders.

Check points

There are key areas of a lease that should be checked when purchasing. Some have already been discussed.

- What is the term left on the lease?
- Is the preamble clear, i.e. is the area which details landlord, tenant and demised (sold) premises, clear?
- Is the lease assignable- i.e. can you pass on the lease without landlords permission or does it need surrendering at sale or a license to assign?
- What is the ground rent and how frequently will you pay it?
- What is the level of service charge, if any, and how is it collected, apportioned, managed and accounted for?
- What are the general restrictions in the lease, can you have pets for example, can you park cars, do you have a designated space?
- What are the respective repairing obligations? As we have seen, the leaseholder will pay anyway but the landlord and leaseholder will hold respective responsibilities. This is an important point because occasionally, there is no stated responsibility for upkeep and the environment deteriorates as a consequence, diminishing the value of the property.

Business leases

Generally, the Landlord and Tenant Act 1954, part 2, provides the framework for those occupying premises on the basis of a business lease. There are a few exceptions to this such as mining leases and agricultural leases. The average business lease will be shorter than a residential lease and will contain periodic rent review clauses. The typical business lease may be for ten years with a rent review after the fifth year.

The whole process of conveyancing business leases, although similar to residential in some respects, is rather more complex. For example, maintenance rights and responsibilities are often an issue between the parties concerned and it is essential that there is a clear picture at the outset. Those coming to the end of the term of their leases can find themselves faced with a significant repair bill, based on a schedule of dilapidations undertaken by a surveyor.

As with all leases, it is very important to ensure that those managing have a firm and comprehensive grasp over the whole process. If they do not then this can affect the value of the property when you wish to sell or buy a lease.

It is not advised that an individual undertakes this type of conveyancing, but employs a solicitor well versed in the finer points of business tenancies. A 'Straightforward Guide to Managing Commercial Property, The Landlord and Tenants Handbook' deals with business tenancies in more depth.

Two systems of conveyancing

After gaining an understanding of the nature of the interest in land that you are buying, it is absolutely essential to understand the two systems of conveyancing property in existence, as this will determine, not so much the procedure because the initial basic steps in conveyancing, such as carrying out searches, are common to both forms of land, registered and unregistered, but the way you go about the process and the final registration.

Registered and unregistered land

In England and Wales the method of conveyancing to be used in each particular transaction very much depends on whether the land is *registered* or *unregistered* land. If the title, or proof of ownership, of land and property has been registered under the Land Registration Acts 1925-86 then the Land Registry (see below) will be able to furnish the would-be conveyancer with such documentation as is required to establish ownership, third party rights etc. If the land has not been registered then proof of ownership of the land in question must be traced through the title deeds.

Registered land

As more and more conveyancing is falling within the remit of the Land Registry, because it is compulsory to register land throughout England and Wales, it is worth outlining this system briefly at this stage. Later on in the book the process of land registration will be covered in more depth.

The Land Registration Acts of 1925 established the Land Registry (HM Land Registry). The Land Registry is a department of the Civil Service, at its head is the Chief Land Registrar. All applications to the Land Registry must be made within the district in question. Anybody can obtain information which is held on the register of a registered title. This has been the case since December 1990.

There is a specific terminology in use within conveyancing, particularly within the land registry:

a) *a piece of land*, or parcel of land is known as a *registered title*
b) the owner of land is referred to as the *registered proprietor*
c) a conveyance of registered land is called *a transfer*
d) a transaction involving registered land is known as *a dealing*

The main difference between the two types of conveyancing *registered* and *unregistered* concerns what is known *as proof of title*. In the case of land that is unregistered the owner will prove title by showing the would-be purchaser the documentary evidence which shows how he or she came to own the land and property.

In the case of registered land the owner has to show simply that he or she is registered at the Land Registry as the registered proprietor. Proof of registration is proof of ownership, which is unequivocal. In registered land the documents proving ownership are replaced by the fact of registration. Each separate title or ownership of land has a title number, which the Land Registry uses to trace ownership, or confirm ownership.

The description of each title on the register is identified by the *title number*, described by reference to the filed plan (indicating limits and extent of ownership). With registered conveyancing the Land Registry keeps the register of title and file plan and title. The owner (proprietor) is issued with a Land Certificate. If the land in question is subject to a mortgage then the mortgagor is issued with a Land Certificate.

Production of the Land Certificate

Before the introduction of the Land Registration Act 2002, with registered land, whenever there is a sale, or disposition, then the Land Certificate had be produced to the Land Registry in the appropriate district. The land Registry no longer produces land or charge certificates.

All forms connected to conveyancing and other advice can be obtained from the Land Registry Website www.land registry.gov.uk

Now please read the key points from chapter one.

KEY POINTS FROM CHAPTER ONE

- Conveyancing is about how to transfer the ownership of land and property from one person to another

- The process of conveyancing lays down clear procedures for the conveyancer and also sets out each party's position during the process

- There are two systems of conveyancing-that dealing with registered land and that dealing with unregistered land. Proof of title is easier to establish when land is registered

- It is compulsory throughout England and Wales to register land-in spite of this more than 30% of land remains unregistered

FRANCES JAMES

KEY STEPS IN CONVEYANCING – THE INITIAL BASIC SEARCHES

THE STRUCTURAL SURVEY

2

THE KEY STEPS IN THE PROCESS OF CONVEYANCING PROPERTY – BASIC SEARCHES

In chapter's three and four, we will be looking specifically at the processes of conveyancing as they affect registered and unregistered land. However, before we do, it is necessary to look at the processes generally, in order to form a clear idea.

Before the buyer exchanges contracts on a property, whether registered or unregistered and then completes the purchase, a number of searches are always carried out. In this chapter we will be looking at four key searches:

- Enquiries before contract
- Local land charges search
- Enquiries of the local authority
- Index map search

These are the most essential and common searches.

Making enquiry's before contract

These are enquiries to the seller, or the Vendor of the property and are aimed at revealing certain facts about the property that the seller has no legal obligation to disclose to the buyer. There are certain matters which are always raised. These are:

a) Whether there are any existing boundary disputes
b) What services are supplied to the property, whether electricity, gas or other
c) Any easements or covenants in the lease. These are stipulations in the lease which give other certain rights, such as rights of way.

d) Any guarantees in existence
f) Planning considerations
g) Adverse rights affecting the property
h) Any fixtures and fittings
i) Whether there has been any breach of restriction affecting the property

If the property is newly built, information will be required concerning any outstanding works or future guarantees of remedying defects. Where a property is leasehold, information will be required about the lessor.

Registered conveyancers will use a standard form to raise these enquiries, so that the initial search is exhaustive. As part of the move towards openness in the process of buying and selling property, and also an attempt to speed up the process of sale, the Law Society has introduced new forms which the solicitor, or buyer if carrying out his or her own conveyancing, is being encouraged to use. These are Seller's Property Information Forms relating to freehold and leasehold property, that the seller and solicitor will respectively fill in, a form relating to fixtures, fittings and contents and a form relating to complete information and requisitions on title.

These forms can be obtained from a legal stationers, such as Oyez and have the pre-fix Prop 1-7. See appendix 1 for examples of these forms.

If a conveyancer is being used then it is advisable to ask whether or not they are using these newly introduced forms. The main point is that you should think long and hard about the type of questions that should be raised. The vendor does not have to answer the questions, but beware a vendor who refuses to disclose answers.

Answers given by the vendor do not form part of the subsequent contract and therefore cannot be used against that person in the event of future problems. However, the

Misrepresentations Act of 1976 could be evoked if a deliberate misrepresentation has caused problems.

Local land charges search

The Local Land Charges Act 1975 requires District Councils, London Borough Councils and the City of London Corporation to maintain a Local Land Charges Registry for the area. Local land charges can be divided into two areas:

a) Financial charges on the land for work carried out by the local authority
b) restrictions on the use of land

The register is further divided into twelve parts:

a) general financial charges
b) specific financial charges
c) planning charges
d) miscellaneous charges and provisions
e) charges for improvements of ways over fenland
f) land compensation charges
g) new town charges
h) civil aviation charges
i) open cast coal mining charges
j) listed buildings charges
k) light obstruction notices
l) drainage scheme charges

All charges are enforceable by the local authority except g and i, which are enforced by statutory bodies and private individuals generally.

A buyer should search in all parts of this particular register and this can be done by a personal or official search. A personal search, as the name suggests, involves the individual or their agent attending at the local authority office and, on paying the relevant fee, personally searching the register. The charges are registered against the land concerned and not against the owner. The official search is the one most favored because, in the event of missing a vital piece of information the chances of compensation are far higher than with a personal search.

With the official search a requisition for a search and for an official certificate of search is sent to the Registrar of Local Land Charges for the area within which the land is situated. There is a fee and the search is carried out by the Registrars staff, which results in a certificate being sent to the person making the request, which clearly outlines any charges.

The Registrar may require a plan of the land as well as the postal address. Separate searches are made of each parcel of land being purchased. Local authority searches

There is a standard form in use for these particular types of searches. This is known as "Con 29 England and Wales" revised April 2000, with the format of the form differing slightly for inner London boroughs. Any of the forms in the process can be obtained from legal stationers such as OYEZ, head office in The Strand London. See appendix for copy.

The standard forms in use contain a statement to the effect that the local authority is not responsible for errors unless negligence is proved. Many of the enquiry's relate specifically to planning matters, whilst other elements of the search are concerned about roads and whether they are adopted and whether there are likely to be any costs falling onto property owners. We will be considering planning matters concerning the individual property a little later. Other enquiry's relate to possible construction of new roads which may affect the property, the location of sewers and pipes and whether the property is in an area of compulsory registration of title, a smoke control area or slum clearance area.

The form used is so constructed that part 2 of the form contains questions, which must be initialed by the purchaser before they are answered. Again these questions cover planning and other matters. Other enquiry's can be asked by the individual, which are answered at the authorities discretion.

In addition to the above, which are the major searches, there are others that the conveyancer has to be aware of. These are as follows:

Searches in the Index map and parcels index of the Land register

If the land has been registered the title will be disclosed and whether it is registered leasehold or freehold. Registered rent charges are also disclosed by the search. (See chapter 7.)

Commons Registration Act (1965) search

This act imposes a duty on County Councils to keep a register relating to village greens and common land and interests over them, such as right of way.

Coal mining search

The request for this search if relevant, is designed to reveal the whereabouts of mineshafts and should be sent to the local Area Coal Board office, or its equivalent. The search will disclose past workings and any subsidence, proposed future workings and the proximity of opencast workings. It is usually well known if there is a problem, or potential problem with coal mining in an area and this search is essential if that is the case.

Other enquiry's

There are a number of other bodies from which it might be appropriate to request a search. These include British Rail, Statutory undertakers such as electricity and gas boards, planning authorities generally, rent assessment committees and so on. These will only usually be necessary if there is a direct link between the property being purchased and a particular circumstance within an area or property.

Planning matters relating to specific properties

It is obviously very necessary to determine whether or not any illegal alterations have been carried out to the property you wish to purchase, before reaching the point of exchange of contracts. This is to ensure that the vendor has complied with relevant planning legislation, if any material changes have been made, and that you will not be required at a later date to carry out remedial work. The Local Authority maintains a register of planning applications relating to properties within their boundaries. In addition, the register will also reveal any planning enforcement notices in force against a particular property.

Questions such as these, and also any questions relating to the effect of Structure or local plans, (specific plans relating to local and borough wide plans for the future) should be made in writing to the local authority or an individual search can be carried out. Usually they are carried out if there is any suspicion that planning regulations may have been breached. In addition, there may be other considerations, such as whether the building is listed or whether tree preservation orders relating to trees within the cartilage of the property are in force. It is certainly essential to know about these.

It is highly recommended that all of these searches are carried out and completed before contracts are exchanged.

Now read the key points from chapter two

KEY POINTS FROM CHAPTER TWO

- Before the buyer exchanges contracts on a property it is essential to carry out a number of key searches

- In addition to the main searches, there are a number of ancillary searches which should be made if appropriate

- There are standard forms for carrying out such searches-if you are doing your own conveyancing these can be obtained from any legal stationers, such as OYEZ in the Strand, London

- There may be other considerations such as conservation or planning issues that need to be looked into.

FRANCES JAMES

3

THE STRUCTURAL SURVEY

Anyone who purchases a property should carry out a structural survey. This is highly advisable and preferably will be as in-depth as possible. A chartered surveyor should be used. If a qualified surveyor is negligent when compiling his or her report of the property then that person can be sued.

As has been stated, it is the aim of the government to move towards a position where the seller has to provide a structural survey of the property being sold. Pilots are currently underway to ascertain the feasibility of this. However, until this becomes law then it is a case of the buyer protecting his or herself.

Most residential property is purchased with assistance from a building society or bank. The lender will insist on a survey before advancing the money in order to protect their advance. However, this survey is cursory at the best and will not reveal more serious problems. Therefore, at this point in the conveyancing process, the person purchasing, or the person acting on his or her behalf should ensure that they are thoroughly acquainted with the condition of the property.

If you are purchasing a house, which is in the course of construction, then there will be the benefit of a warranty of good work and proper materials so that the house will be fit for habitation. This protection does not extend to any subsequent purchasers.

There is however, a form of Statutory protection under the Defective Premises Act of 1972 which imposes a duty on a developer and those associated with the developer to build in a correct manner. The Act covers anyone acquiring an interest in a dwelling

The National House builders Scheme

This scheme was redrafted in 1979 and in 1988 the Buildmark scheme was introduced. Builders who are registered with the NHBC must offer a warranty to first and subsequent purchasers, that, essentially, has a ten-year shelf life from date of construction. During the first two years from issue the builder is liable to make good any defects due to non-compliance with NHBC regulations. The first two years are known as the initial guarantee period. After this, the remaining eight years are referred to as the structural guarantee period. During this time the NHBC will reimburse the purchaser the cost of remedying major works caused by any defect in the structure or subsidence, settlement or heave, provided that there is no other insurance at the time of the claim to cover the cost.

Liability of the builder outside the two year period

The NHBC agreement states that if any work undertaken by the builder in the initial guarantee period to remedy a defect caused by the breach of the NHBC requirements fails to remedy the defect or damage, the vendor/builder will remain under a continuing liability to remedy the damage after the initial guarantee period.

Conveyancing a property is not just about successfully reaching a conclusion in a sale. It is also about ensuring that the property you are buying is sound and that you make sure that you have a clear picture of what you are buying, preferably by obtaining a report from a chartered surveyor.

Now read the key points from chapter three

4

CONVEYANCING UNREGISTERED LAND – THE MAIN PROCESSES PRIOR TO EXCHANGE AND COMPLETION OF A SALE OF PROPERTY

We have considered the processes of conveyancing generally and the searches common to all property. However, it is now necessary to look at the specifics of conveyancing registered and unregistered land.

With unregistered land, as we have seen, there is a duty on the vendor to prove his or her title to the land, i.e., that they own the land in question. If all is registered at the Land Registry then life can be a good deal simpler. However, if not, then the process can be more complex.

The abstract of title - unregistered land. Establishing proof of ownership

The abstract of title is an epitome of the various documents and events which together demonstrate that the vendor has good title to the land, conclusively owns the land. The vendor must, at his or her own expense, produce and deliver a proper abstract of title to the purchaser, unless there is an agreement to do otherwise, which would be unusual.

The abstract starts with the root, or the origin of title. Every deed which dealt with transactions relating to this property subsequently, must be abstracted. A conveyance relating to the purchase of the freehold is the strongest form of root of title, likewise a mortgage deed relating to that conveyance. If a vendor has lost any of the titles which relate to the land then it is usual for the vendor to insert a special condition into the contract stating what secondary evidence will be produced to prove title. Secondary evidence can be in the form of a counterpart lease, for example.

Once the abstract has been delivered, the purchaser must examine these documents against the originals. The purpose of the examination is to ensure that what has been abstracted has been properly or correctly abstracted, ensure that each document has been properly executed, attested and stamped and that there have been no changes to the title, such as memoranda endorsed on deeds or documents. Any doubt as to the validity of the title should be raised with the vendor's solicitor directly and promptly by written requisition. The purchaser is entitled to raise requisitions on any part of the title, which is unsatisfactory, for example, if the title discloses a mortgage, or covenant, which was not disclosed in the contract. An omission from the abstract may be remedied by an answer to the requisition. The expense of verification of this answer is the purchaser's. The purchaser can serve a notice on the vendor requiring him to furnish an answer by a given date. Failure to reply by this date entitles the purchaser to rescind the contract. If the purchaser is still not satisfied within the vendor's replies, he or she can send observations back to the vendor relating to the reply.

There is a standard condition of sale, which states that the vendor can rescind the sale if he or she cannot furnish a reasonable reply to the requisition. This right however, is based on reasonable grounds, i.e., inability or unwillingness to answer.

Searches to be carried out prior to completion

We discussed the key searches to be carried out prior to exchange and completion in the previous chapter. There are, however, other searches necessary, depending on the status of the property. With unregistered property, some of these searches involve the Land Registry.

The purchaser or agent should carry out various searches immediately before completion in order to determine whether there are any encumbrances affecting the vendor's title to the property. The most important of these is the Land Charges register of the Land Charges Department of the Land Registry.

There are five registers in total:

a) the register of pending actions. This registers any actions that may be pending against that title.

b) the register of annuities. This registers any rent charge or other charge such as an annuity against the land

c) the registry of writs and orders. This register is concerned with the registering and enforcing of any orders against land.

d) The register of deeds and arrangements. This is concerned with trustees or creditors who may benefit from that particular title.

e) The register of land charges.

The Register of Land charges

This is the most important register and the charges are classified as follows:

a) Class A (s. 2(2). These are charges upon land, created by statute, which only come into existence after the appropriate person has made an application under the particular statute. Once created they may be registered against the estate owner.

b) Class B (s 2 (3)). These are similar charges to those in class A.

c) Class C is subdivided as follows.

i) a puisne mortgage, i.e., a legal mortgage not being protected by the deposit of documents relating to the legal estate affected.

a limited owner's charge, an equitable charge acquired by a tenant for life by a statutory owner by statute because he has paid taxes or other liability related to the estate.

ii) A general equitable charge. This is a sweeping up charge, including all charges not protected by the deposit of title deeds etc.

iii) An estate contract. This is an estate contract by someone who is entitled at the date of contract to have the legal estate conveyed to him, to convey or create a legal estate.

d) Class D, this is a charge on land acquired by the commissioners of the Inland Revenue for unpaid capital transfer taxes

e) Class E .This class covers annuities

f) Class F covers charges affecting the matrimonial home by virtue of a spouses rights of occupation under the Matrimonial Homes Act 1983 as amended by the Family Law Act 1996.

Methods of making a land charges search

A search may be made in person, by post, by telex or by telephone. Personal searches should not be made as this should be left to those who know the system and are employed to carry out searches.

A postal search effective for all registers is made on a form PIC. The information required for a postal search is the name of the estate owner, period of years searched against, address, county and description of property. Completed searches are usually sent back promptly. If the search reveals an adverse entry then the purchaser should ensure that property concerned is not affected.

Other searches

Company searches are usually necessary if the property to be purchased is from a company. Company agents can ascertain whether there is a winding up order against the company or whether there are any specific charges relating to that company registered against the title to land.

The nature of the conveyance

It should be noted that, if land to be conveyed is in an area of compulsory registration at the Land Registry, as most land is, the purchasers solicitor may, instead of preparing the traditional form of conveyance as described below, utilize the much simpler form of a registered land transfer. For more details concerning this form see chapter 5. For those whose property will not be immediately registered the following applies.

The purchaser's solicitor will prepare a draft conveyance in duplicate and sends it to the vendor's solicitor for scrutiny and approval. The vendor's solicitor will normally send back a copy with amendments in red pen. When the deed is agreed (settled) the purchasers solicitor has it engrossed (fair copied) and then sends it to the vendors solicitor to keep until the day of completion.

The contents of a typical conveyance of unregistered land

An example conveyance is shown further on in this chapter. The heading of the document will begin with the words "This conveyance or "This deed of gift" etc. The conveyance is dated and the full names of the parties are inserted along with their addresses. If there are parties other than the vendor and purchaser, for example, any trustees, they are also inserted.

The Recital

This part of the deed will usually begin "whereas" and the purpose is to outline a history of transactions related to that property. They are largely unnecessary and are there as a result of tradition as it as evolved in conveyancing.

The Testatum

The testatum is part of the operative part of the conveyance and will begin with "Now this deed witnesses"

The formal words are followed by a statement of consideration for the transaction and a receipt by the vendor for the purchase money. No other receipt is required, although this does not stop a vendor challenging the fact that a receipt has been paid.

Words of grant

These are the words, which pass the vendors estate to the purchaser. The usual form of words will state "The vendor as beneficial owner hereby conveys". There will then be a description of the property conveyed, known as the parcels clause.

In a lease there will be what is known as a reddendum, which goes on to describe rent and rent days.

There are also what is known as covenants, either negative or positive covenants, which impose obligations, or rights on either party. In modern developments these conveyances are usually very lengthy and are contained in a schedule to the deed.

Where a vendor remains liable on a covenant after sale he or she should ensure that the purchaser enters into a covenant to indemnify the vendor in respect of any liability arising from a future breach of that covenant. The effect is to indemnify the vendor against any loss or expenses in respect of breach of covenant.

Where the property is conveyed to joint tenants a clause is very often included declaring that each tenant holds joint equity and conferring on the co-owners additional powers of dealing with the land in question.

The testimonium

This is the formal clause, which precedes the party's execution of the deed and will typically be worded " IN WITNESS whereof the parties hereto have executed this document as their deed the day and year first before mentioned"

Execution of deeds before July 31st 1990

The Law of Property Act 1989 introduced very important changes in the execution of deeds. Under the Law of Property Act 1925 three formal requirements for a deed are outlined, namely that it must be signed sealed and delivered. The effective date of the deed is the effective date of delivery. However, after 1989 a seal is no longer required, just an effective signature, signed before a witness. The Companies Act 1989 also allows for companies to execute a deed by signature, with a seal no longer a requirement.

Completion of sale of unregistered land

The date for completion will be stated in the contract. See chapter 6. Usually, completion will take place at the offices of the vendor's solicitor. If there is an outstanding mortgage on the property and the mortgagee will not release the deeds to the vendors solicitor until after it is discharged then completion will take place at the mortgagees solicitor.

Completion allows for settling of the financial account between vendor and purchaser and completion of legal work plus handing over the executed deed. Money is usually sent from a bank to the solicitor. Deeds are usually examined a last time to see that all is correct. The vendor may retain part of a title deed if there is any ongoing involvement, i.e., part ownership of land etc.

In unregistered conveyancing the legal estate is vested in the purchaser. The purchaser is also entitled to possession of the property and the solicitors should ensure that adequate arrangements have been made to this end.

Where the vendor is selling as a personal representative of another, a memoranda of sale should be endorsed on the grant of representation which he or she will have. Where the purchaser enters into covenants for the protection of land retained or is granted additional rights, such as rights over land, it is common for the vendor to retain a duplicate copy (counterpart).

Example conveyance of unregistered land

This CONVEYANCE BY DEED is made the seventh day of July Two Thousand and Six between J Smith of 19 Jupiter Street, Othertown (hereinafter called the vendor) of one part and F Deal of 1 Mars Street Eithertown (hereinafter called the purchaser) of the other part

---

WHEREAS

(1) The vendor is seised of the property hereinafetr described for an estate in fee simple in possession free from encumbrances and as hereinafter mentioned and has agreed with the purchaser for the sale to him of the said property for a like estate for a price of seventy five thousand pounds

NOW THIS DEED WITNSSETH

1._____ In pursuance of the said agreement and in consideration of the sum of seventy five thousand pounds now paid by the purchaser to the vendor (the receipt of which sum the vendor hereby acknowledges) the vendor as beneficial owner hereby conveys unto the purchaser all that land and property known as 41 Otherplace, Othertown as was conveyed to the vendor by John Rarer by a conveyance of 25th May 1952 and is further therein more particularly described and subject to the covenants therein contained but otherwise free from encumbrances TO HOLD the same unto the purchaser in fee simple_____

2. With the object and intent of affording to the vendor a full and sufficient indemnity but not further or otherwise the purchaser hereby covenants with the vendor to observe and perform the above mentioned covenant and to indemnify the vendor against all actions claims demands and liabilities in respect thereof _____

3. It is hereby certified that the transaction affected does not form part of a larger transaction or of a series of transactions in respect of which the amount or value or the aggregate amount or value of the consideration exceeds eighty pounds_____

___IN WITNESS whereof the parties hereto have executed this document as their deed the day and year first before written.

EXECUTED AS HIS DEED
By the aforementioned
J Smith in the presence of   ) J Smith
K Knowles   )
46 hilltop   )
Otherplace

EXECUTED AS HIS DEED
By the aforementioned
John Rarer in the presence of   ) John Rarer
K Smile   )
42 Child Street
Cidertown   )
Now read the key points from chapter 4

KEY POINTS FROM CHAPTER FOUR

- The purchasers solicitor will prepare a draft in conveyance in duplicate and send in duplicate to the vendors solicitor for scrutiny and approval

- When the deal is agreed, the purchasers solicitor has it engrossed and then sends it to the vendors solicitor to until completion

- Deeds executed after July 31st 1990 do not require a seal

- The date for completion should be clearly stated in the contract

- Completion allows for the settling of the financial account between vendor and purchaser

REGISTERED LAND - PROOF OF TITLE AND OTHER SEARCHES

FRANCES JAMES

5

CONVEYANCING REGISTERED LAND – PROCESSES PRIOR TO COMPLETION

In chapter 4, we looked at the general process of conveyancing unregistered land. In this chapter we will concentrate on registered land.

First Registration of title

First registration of land may take place voluntarily or compulsorily depending on the nature of the transaction. Land Registry Form FR1 should be used. Compulsory registration now extends to most of England and Wales. It is highly undesirable to complete a sale of land and then neglect to register it. When a sale is completed an application must be lodged for registration within two months of completion. The effect of non-registration is that the deed of transfer, or the conveyance, becomes null and void after the two-month period. In other words, there is no choice but to register the land.

Under s123 of the Law of Property Act, the Chief Land Registrar may accept a late registration. An explanation of why the property was not registered within the time period will be required. Acceptance of the application has the effect of registering the estate to the purchaser from the date of completion. Late applications are rarely refused.

When land is purchased in a compulsory area but the title is not yet registered, even where the transaction must be followed by a first registration the procedure until completion is identical to the procedure in unregistered conveyancing. The purchaser will know that he must effect a first registration from the form 96 search of the index map, as outlined. In addition the reply to one of the standard enquiries of the district council within which the land is situated will reveal whether or not the land is in an area of compulsory registration. In effect, as stated, most land is in an area of compulsory registration.

The purchaser's solicitor will forward the correct form to the land registry. For a first registration of freehold land form 1A is used.

This form is called a "cover" because it is double sided and when folded will contain all the necessary documentation for registration. The cover will contain a certificate signed by a solicitor that the title has been properly investigated, a statement that any land charges entries revealed by the official search either do or do not affect the land concerned and if they do a note of the document by which they were created. In addition, a schedule of encumbrances affecting the property is sent.

All the original deeds and other documents of title must be sent. Enough information by way of plan must be sent to enable Registry staff to fix the position of the property on the Ordnance Survey Map. There is a prescribed fee which the Land Registry can provide details of on request.

For application by the owner for first registration of leasehold land other than on the grant of a new lease and for application by the owner for first registration of leasehold land on grant of a new lease, see appendix for forms.

Outline of the Land Registry and the registration process
As discussed earlier in the book, the essential difference between registered and unregistered land is that unregistered land requires production of deeds to land as proof of title. Registered conveyancing entails the owner quite simply demonstrating that the registered proprietorship is recorded at the Land Registry.

In registered land the documents of title are replaced by the fact of registration. Therefore, the equivalent to the title deed is the various entries in the Land Registry.

Each title is given a title number, which is then used to trace title. The description of each title is identified by a title number, described by reference to a filed plan and a set of index cards retained to record specifics about that title.

The index cards and the filed plan are the equivalent of title deeds. The registered proprietor is issued with a land certificate containing a facsimile copy of the registered title. If land within a particular title number is subject to a mortgage the land certificate is retained by the Registry and the mortgagee is instead issued with a charge certificate, and the land certificate is retained by the Land Registry.

There are three registers of title at the Land Registry, the Property Register, The Proprietorship Register and the Charges Register.

The Property Register is similar to the Parcels Clause in unregistered conveyancing i.e. it describes the land in question. It will identify the geographical location and extent of the registered property by means of a short description and a reference to an official plan, which is prepared for each title. It may also give particulars of any rights that benefit the land, for example, a right of way over adjoining land. In the case of a lease the register will also describe the parties to the lease, the term and the rent, any exceptions or reservations from the lease and, if the lessors title is registered, the title number.

The Proprietorship Register is similar to the Habendum in unregistered conveyancing. It will describe the type of title, i.e., title absolute, leasehold etc, the full name and address of the registered proprietor, description of that person, date of registration, price paid for the property and any other relevant entries. There will also be any relevant cautions, inhibitions or restrictions entered on the Register.

The Charges Register contains any encumbrances affecting the registered property, such as mortgages and any other charges taken over the property. However, details of amount of money involved are not disclosed.

How to inspect the Register

The Land Registry has developed an e conveyancing system, online. At the moment, the best and most convenient way of obtaining details from the register is by post on Land Registry form PIC for a copy of the Register entries and/or a copy of the title plan if required. One form is required for each registered title inspected. A fee will be payable. If you do not have the title number the Land Registry will, for a fee, search for the number.

If you wish, after you have received the copies of the register that you require, you can, by filling in the appropriate forms (see appendix 1) obtain for copies of documents that you would like to inspect. Again, a fee is payable. If you only wish to know the name and address of the registered proprietor of a property, you should fill in Land Registry form PN1 and send it to:

The Customer Information Centre, Room 105, The Harrow District Land Registry, Lyon House, Harrow, Middlesex HA1 2EU. A list of Land Registry fees can be obtained from this address.

The Land or Charge Certificate

When a title is registered for the first time or changes hands, a Land Certificate was issued by the Land Registry. The Land Certificate was regarded as the equivalent to the title deed although this can be misleading as it is only a facsimile of the official register and may not be up to date. In addition, there may be matters of title not contained on the register. The Land Certificate had to be produced to the appropriate Land registry whenever there was a sale or transfer of land. A Charge Certificate had to be produced too.

As mentioned in the introduction, following the introduction of the land Registration Act 2002, Land and Charge Certificates have now been abolished. If you have lost your certificate you do not need to replace it.

Maps and descriptions of land

The Index map and parcels index provides that a map should be kept showing the position and extent of all registered titles. This is called the Public Index Map. This is open to inspection by any person, and can be inspected personally or by official search (see appendix). There will be a fee for this search.

All registered land must, in addition, be described by the applicant in such a way as to enable the land to be fully identified on the ordnance map or general map.

The Land Registry uses a consistent colour coding on its plans. This does not vary and it is expected that solicitors when preparing plans will use the same system. The colouring scheme is as follows: Red edging marks the extent of land within a particular title. Green edging marks land removed from a title. Green tinting shows excluded pieces of land within the area of the title

1. Brown tinting shows land over which the registered land has a right of way.

2. Blue tinting shows land within the title subject to a right of way.

3. For further references, colours are used in the following order:

a) tinting in pink, blue yellow and mauve;
b) edging with a blue yellow or mauve band;
c) hatching with a colour other than black or green;
d) numbering or lettering of small self contained areas.

In addition, when reading a filed plan it should be noted that a boundary represented by a feature shown on the ground or on the existing ordnance survey is represented by a continuous dark line. A boundary not representing such a feature is shown by a broken dark line.

The scale of the filed plan is usually 1/1250 enlarged from the survey 1/2500.

KEY POINTS FROM CHAPTER FIVE

- Registered conveyancing entails the owner simply demonstrating that the registered proprietorship is recorded at the Land Registry

- Each title is given a title number, which is described by reference to a filed plan and a set of Index Cards. These are the equivalent of title deeds

- There are three registers of title at the Land Registry, The Property Register, The Proprietorship Register and The Charges Register

- The best and most convenient way of obtaining details from the Register is by post on Land Registry form number 109

- First registration of land may take place voluntarily or be compulsory depending on the nature of the transaction.

FRANCES JAMES

THE CONTRACT FOR SALE – EXCHANGE AND COMPLETION

6

THE CONTRACT FOR SALE

Forming the contract

Having discussed the processes involved in conveying registered and unregistered land, prior to exchange and completion, it is now necessary to look at the contract for sale, which is formulated at the outset but not exchanged or completed before all parties are satisfied with the prior processes of conveyancing.

As with many other transactions, a sale of land is effected through a contract. However, a contract, which deals with the sale of land, is governed by the requirements of the Law of Property (miscellaneous provisions) Act 1989, the equitable doctrine of specific performance and the duty of the vendor to provide title to the property.

The Law of Property Act (Miscellaneous provisions) 1988 provides that contracts dealing with the sale of land after 26th September 1989 must be in writing. The contract must contain all the terms and agreements to which the respective parties to the transaction have agreed. The provisions of the Act do not apply to sales at a public auction, contracts to grant a short lease and contracts regulated under the Financial Services Act 1986. If the person purchasing is doing so through an agent then the agent must have authority to act on behalf of the purchaser. Examples of agents are auctioneers and solicitors, also estate agents.

Agreements which are subject to contract and also conditional agreements

If the phrase "subject to contract" is used in a sale then the intention of both parties to the contract is that neither are contractually bound until a formal contract has been agreed by the parties, signed and exchanged. Therefore, the words "subject to contract" are a protective device, although it is not good to depend on the use of these words throughout a transaction

Procedures in the formation of contract

The vendor's solicitor will usually draw up an initial contract of sale. This is because only this person has access to all the necessary initial documents to begin to effect a contract. The draft contract is prepared in two parts and sent to the purchaser's solicitor (if using a solicitor); the other side will approve or amend the contract as necessary. Both sides must agree to any proposed amendments. After agreement has been reached, the vendor's solicitor will retain one copy of the contract and send the other copy to the solicitor or person acting for the other side. The next stage is for the vendors solicitor to engross (sign and formalize) the contract in two parts. Both parts are then sent to the purchaser's solicitor or other agent who checks that they are correct then sends one part back to the vendor's solicitor.

Signing the contract

The vendors solicitor will obtain the vendors signature to the contract, when he is satisfied that the vendor can sell what he is purporting to do through the contract. The purchaser's solicitor or agent will do the same, having checked the replies to all enquiries before contract. It is also essential to check that a mortgage offer has been made and accepted.

Exchanging contracts

Neither party to the sale is legally bound until there has been an exchange of contracts. At one time, a face-to-face exchange would have taken place. However, with the rapid increases in property transactions this rarely happen nowadays. Exchange by post is more common. The purchaser will post his or her part of the contract together with the appropriate cheque to cover the agreed deposit, to the purchaser's solicitor or person acting on behalf of that Person. The purchaser's solicitor will usually insert the agreed completion date. On receiving this part of the contract the vendor will add his or her part and send this off in exchange. At this stage, both parties become bound under the contract.

A contract to convey or create an estate in land is registrable as a class C (IV) land charge, an estate contract. You should take further advice on this, as it is not current practice to do so.

The Contents of a contract

A contract will be in two parts, *the particulars of sale* and the *conditions of sale*. The particulars of sale give a physical description of the land and also of the interest, which is being sold. A property must be described accurately and a plan may be attached to the contract to emphasize or illustrate what is in the contract. The particulars will also outline whether the property is freehold or leasehold and what kind of lease the vendor is assigning, i.e., head lease (where vendor is owner of the freehold) or underlease, where the vendor is not.

It is very important to determine what kind of lease it is that is being assigned, indeed whether it is assignable or whether permission is needed from the landlord and it is recommended that a solicitor handle this transaction. This is because any purchaser of a lease can find his or her interest jeopardized by the nature of the lease. Where a sub-lease, or under lease is being purchased, the purchasers interest can be forfeited by the actions of the head lessee, the actions of this person being out of control of the purchaser.

Rights, such as easements and also restrictive covenants, which are for the benefit of the land, should be expressly referred to in the particulars of sale. In addition, the vendor should refer to any latent defects affecting his or her property, if known. This includes any encumbrances, which may affect the property.

Misdescription

If the property in the particulars of sale is described wrongly, i.e. there is a misstatement of fact, such as describing leasehold as freehold land, calling an under-lease a lease or leaving out something that misleads the buyer, in other words, if the mis description is material, then the purchaser is entitled to rescind the contract. Essentially the contract must describe what is being sold and if it does not, and the buyer is mislead then the contract is inaccurate.

If the misdescription is immaterial and insubstantial, and there has been no misrepresentation then the purchaser cannot rescind the contract. However, if the misdescription has affected the purchase price of the property then the purchaser can insist on a reduction in the asking price. The purchaser should claim this compensation before completion takes place.

The vendor has no right to rescind the contract if the misdescription is in the purchaser's favor, for example, the area of land sold is greater than that intended. Neither can the vendor compel the purchaser to pay an increased purchase price

Misrepresentation

Misrepresentation is an untrue statement of fact made by one party or his or her agent, which induces the other party to enter into the contract. An opinion and a statement of intention must be distinguished from a statement of fact. There are three types of misrepresentation, fraudulent misrepresentation, negligent misrepresentation and innocent misrepresentation. Fraudulent misrepresentation is a false statement made knowingly or without belief in its truth, or recklessly. The innocent party may sue through the tort of negligence either before or after the contract is complete and rescind the contract.

Negligent misrepresentation, although not fraudulent, is where the vendor or his or her agents cannot prove that the statement they made in relation to the contract was correct. Remedies available are damages or rescission of the contract. Innocent misrepresentation is where the statement made was neither fraudulently or negligently but is still an untrue statement. Rescission is available for this particular type of misrepresentation.

Rescission of contract generally is available under the Misrepresentation Act 1967 s 2(2).

Non-disclosure

Generally, in the law of contract, there is the principle of "caveat emptor" "let the buyer beware". In other words, it is up to the purchaser to ensure that what he or she is buying is worth the money paid for it. Earlier we talked about the importance of searches and also, particularly, the importance of the structural survey. Although the vendor has some responsibility to reveal any defects in the property it is always very advisable for the purchaser to ensure that all checks prior to purchase are carried out thoroughly.

Conditions of sale

There are two types of conditions, special conditions and general conditions. Special conditions are those which are specific to an individual contract, such as when a specific day is fixed for completion. The general conditions are those which have general application.

General conditions of sale are standard entitled, "National protocol for domestic leasehold and freehold property." This is a complete guide to conveyancing in itself and can be obtained from the Law Society.

The general conditions of sale oblige the vendor to supply the purchaser with abstracts or any copies of a lease or agreement in writing. The vendor must always supply the purchaser with details of any tenancy agreements in existence. A deposit for the purchase will only be payable if there is a special or general condition to this effect, such a term is not implied into a contract. Under standard conditions a deposit of 10% of the purchase price is paid to the vendors solicitor prior to purchase but this can be varied between parties. The deposit should be in cash or by banker's draft at the date of the contract (exchange). Failure to pay, or payment by a cheque, which is subsequently dishonored, is a breach and can lead to the vendor rescinding the contract. The general conditions specifically refer to this.

If there is any interest due, or expected on purchase money this will be dealt with in the special conditions of contract.

Completion

The requirements concerning completion are detailed thoroughly in the general conditions of sale. Payment on completion is one such detail. Payment on completion should be by one of the following methods:

a) legal tender;
b) bankers draft;
c) an unconditional authority to release any deposit by the stakeholder
d) any other method agreed with the vendor.

At common law, completion takes place whenever the vendor wishes and payment is to be made by legal tender.

Also dealt with in the general conditions is failure to complete and notices to complete. Failure to complete can cause difficulty for one of the other parties and the aggrieved party can serve notice on the other to complete by a specific date. The notice has the effect of making "time of the essence" which means that a specific date is attached to completion, after which the contract is discharged.

Return of pre contract deposits

The vendor must return any deposit paid to the purchaser if the purchaser drops out before the exchange of contracts. This cannot be prevented and was the subject of a House of Lords ruling in the 1977 case Sorrel v Finch.

The position of the parties after exchange of contracts

Once a contract has been exchanged the purchaser is the beneficial owner of the property, with the vendor owning the property on trust for the purchaser. The vendor is entitled to any rents or other profits from the land during this period, has the right to retain the property until final payments have been made and has a lien (charge/right) over the property in respect of any unpaid purchase monies.

The vendor is bound to take reasonable care of the property and should not let the property fall into disrepair or other damages to be caused during the period between exchange and completion. If completion does not take place at the allotted time and the fault is the purchasers then interest can be charged on the money due.

The purchaser, as beneficial owner of the property is entitled to any increase in the value of the land and buildings but not profits arising. The purchaser has a right of lien over the property, the same as the vendor, in respect of any part of the purchase price paid prior to completion.

Bankruptcy of the vendor

In the unfortunate event of the vendor going bankrupt in between exchange and completion, the normal principles of bankruptcy apply so that the trustee in bankruptcy steps in to the vendor's shoes. The purchaser can be compelled to complete the sale. The trustee in bankruptcy is obliged to complete the sale if the purchaser tenders the purchase money on the completion day.

Bankruptcy of the purchaser

When a purchaser is declared bankrupt in between sale and completion all of his or her property vests in the trustee in bankruptcy. The trustee can compel the vendor to complete the transaction by paying monies due by the allotted day. If the vendor wishes to proceed with the sale and the trustee is reluctant, the trustee has the right to claim that the contract is onerous. However, in these circumstances, the vendor can keep any deposit due to him. A form for bankruptcy purchases is shown in appendix 1.

Death of Vendor or purchaser

The personal representatives of a deceased vendor can compel the purchaser to sell. The money is conveyed to those representatives who will hold the money in accordance with the terms of any will or in accordance with the rules relating to intestacy if there is no will.

The same position applies to the purchaser's representatives, who can be compelled by the vendor to complete the purchase and who can hold money on the purchaser's behalf.

Now read the key points from chapter six.

KEY POINTS FROM CHAPTER SIX

- As with many other transactions, a sale of land is affected through a contract. The Law of Property Act, (Miscellaneous Provisions) 1988 provides that contracts dealing with the sale of land after 26th September 1989, must be in writing

- If the phrase "subject to contract" is used then the intention of both parties to the contract is that neither are contractually bound until a formal contract has been agreed, signed and exchanged by the parties

- Neither party is legally bound until there has been an exchange of contracts

- Contracts are in two parts, The Particulars of Sale and the Conditions of Sale. The particulars give a physical description of the land and interest. There are two types of conditions, special and general. The latter is governed by the National Protocol for Domestic Leasehold and Freehold Property

FRANCES JAMES

7

POST COMPLETION REGISTERED AND UNREGISTERED LAND

Completion of a land transaction will usually happen in the office of the vendor's solicitor. If there is an outstanding mortgage on the property and the mortgagee will not release the deeds to until after payment has been made then completion will take place in the mortgagee's solicitors premises.

Completion will entail settling any outstanding payments between the vendor and purchaser. Also any legal work will be completed and deeds, if appropriate will be handed over.

On every transfer of sale of a freehold, lease or under-lease of seven years or more, the purchaser must complete a form giving particulars to the Inland Revenue. The form is to register the property for stamp duty and is known as "Stamps 1 (A) 451" or the "Particulars Delivered" form.

If the land is registered or being registered for the first time after completion, then if there is no stamp duty land tax (SDLT) payable the particulars must be sent to the Land Registry together with an application for registration. In every other case, the deed and the particulars delivered form must be sent to the Inland Revenue within thirty days of completion. Currently stamp duty land tax stands at 1% of the value of the property over £120,001, £120,000 to £250,000 1%, £250,001 to £500,000 3% and £500,001 and above 4%. There are some areas designated as disadvantaged areas and they will have a nil rate up to £150,000. You should always check with estate agents and solicitors when buying a property.

An application must be made to the Land Registry to register the transaction. This will involve sending:

1. The fee
2. The transfer form TR1 which is used in all cases where the transfer of a title has happened.
3. Evidence of any previous mortgage being paid off.
4. Details of the new charge by the delivery of a copy of the mortgage and original mortgage.

The title can then be registered in the name of the new purchaser together with details of any new charge.

Once registration is complete a copy should be sent to the purchaser for checking and any original documents should be sent to the lender for safekeeping.

CONCLUSION

This book is intended to be a guide to the processes of conveyancing and should be used in conjunction with a solicitor.

The book is very much about the procedures involved in buying and selling property. However, unless a conveyance is likely to be straightforward then you are advised to employ a solicitor or licensed conveyancer to carry out the work. Prices for such work are quite often very competitive and if there is a problem along the way then at least you have redress after the event.

Summary of process

We saw in chapter two that there are basic searches common to all properties that must be carried out prior to exchange of contracts. In chapter three we discussed the importance of carrying out a structural survey before committing to a purchase. In chapter four we discussed the various issues concerning unregistered land and the need to prove title and to carry out further additional searches. In chapter five we discussed the issues surrounding registered land and proof of title. Finally we discussed the contract for sale and process of completion following the various stages of conveyancing of land.

A few simple words of advice:

When buying property make sure that all debts are paid by the vendor before completing. This is especially pertinent to leasehold property that is quite often subject to a service charge. If the vendor does not settle debts then the purchaser will find his or herself taking on the debt. *Read contracts/leases very carefully indeed.* Make sure that you know what it is that you are buying and that you are fully aware. *Buying and selling property is a complex task*-be very cautious and always scrutinise all documents very carefully. Make sure that what you buy is in sound condition and represents a good investment. It is the biggest investment that you will probably make.

GLOSSARY OF TERMS

ABSTRACT
(Of Title) This is the evidence that a person selling his or her property will produce during the process of sale.

ASSENT
A document by which personal representatives convey property to the person entitled to the property which is part of a deceased estate that they are administering.

CAUTION
An entry on the title of registered land notifying that someone claiming an interest is entitled to notice of dealing.

CHARGE
In registered conveyancing a registered charge is a mortgage protected by entry on the register of the mortgaged property.

CONVEYANCE
A deed transferring the legal estate in land

COUNTERPART (Lease)
An exact copy of the deed to be used when the deed is to be executed in duplicate so that each party will have an original.

DEALING
A transaction with registered title

ENCUMBRANCE
An interest adverse to a particular legal or equitable estate, for example a mortgage.

ENGROSSMENT
The fair copy which is to be used as the actual deed.

EPITOME
Lists of documents of title in chronological order stating the date, type of document and parties and whether or not the vendor will retain the original on completion.

HABENDUM
The part of the deed that shows how the purchaser is to hold the land.

INHIBITION
An entry on the title of registered land preventing any dealing with the land being registered.

MEMORANDUM
A note on a deed or other instrument recording some dealing with the land or estate to which that instrument is pertinent, or some written evidence of a contract for sale.

RECITAL
An introductory part of a deed telling the story of the transaction or the title concerned.

ROOT OF TITLE
The deed or event from which in unregistered conveyancing the vendor undertakes to trace his title.

STATUTORY DECLARATION
A declaration under oath in accordance with the Statutory Declarations Act 1835. Used in conveyancing, for example, to explain lost or stolen deeds or any other defects in title.

TESTIMONIUM
A formal introduction to the attestation clause in a deed.

TRANSFER

A conveyance of registered land.

TRANSMISSION

The passing of registered title on the death or bankruptcy of the registered proprietor.

INDEX

APPENDIX 1

Some of the important Land Registry forms used in the basic processes of conveyancing. For a complete list contact your local Land Registry or a legal stationers, such as OYEZ. Copies can also be downloaded on the internet.

Address of the Property:

1. Place a tick in one of these three columns against every item.

2. The second column ("excluded from the sale") is for items on the list which you are proposing to take with you when you move. If you are prepared to sell any of these to the buyer, please write the price you wish to be paid beside the name of the item and the buyer can then decide whether or not to accept your offer to sell.

	INCLUDED IN THE SALE	EXCLUDED FROM THE SALE	NONE AT THE PROPERTY
TV Aerial/Satellite Dish			
Radio Aerial			
Immersion Heater			
Hot Water Cylinder Jacket			
Roof Insulation			
Wall Heaters			
Night Storage Heater			
Gas/Electric Fires with any surround			
Light Fittings:			
Ceiling Lights	☐	☐	☐
Wall Lights	☐	☐	☐
Lamp Shades	☐	☐	☐
N.B. If these are to be removed, it is assumed that they will be replaced by ceiling rose and socket, flex, bulb holder and bulb.			
Switches			
Electric Points			
Dimmer Switches			
Fluorescent Lighting			
Outside Lights			

This form comprises 6 pages. Please ensure you complete all sections on all pages. Please turn over to next page.

Prop 6/1

Peapod Solutions Limited is an Approved Law Society Supplier

Peapod Solutions Ltd.

	INCLUDED IN THE SALE	EXCLUDED FROM THE SALE	NONE AT THE PROPERTY
Telephone Receivers:			
British Telecom	☐	☐	☐
Own	☐	☐	☐
Burglar Alarm System			
Complete Central Heating System			
Extractor Fans			
Doorbell/Chimes			
Door Knocker			
Door Furniture:			
Internal	☐	☐	☐
External	☐	☐	☐
Double Glazing			
Window Fitments			
Shutters/Grills			
Curtain Rails			
Curtain Poles			
Pelmets			
Venetian Blinds			
Roller Blinds			
Curtains (Including Net Curtains):			
Lounge	☐	☐	☐
Dining Room	☐	☐	☐
Kitchen	☐	☐	☐
Bathroom	☐	☐	☐

	INCLUDED IN THE SALE	EXCLUDED FROM THE SALE	NONE AT THE PROPERTY
Bedroom 1	☐	☐	☐
Bedroom 2	☐	☐	☐
Bedroom 3	☐	☐	☐
Bedroom 4	☐	☐	☐
Other Rooms (state which)			
1	☐	☐	☐
2	☐	☐	☐
3	☐	☐	☐
Carpets and other Floor Covering:			
Lounge	☐	☐	☐
Dining Room	☐	☐	☐
Kitchen	☐	☐	☐
Hall, Stairs and Landing	☐	☐	☐
Bathroom	☐	☐	☐
Bedroom 1	☐	☐	☐
Bedroom 2	☐	☐	☐
Bedroom 3	☐	☐	☐
Bedroom 4	☐	☐	☐
Other Rooms (state which)			
1	☐	☐	☐
2	☐	☐	☐
3	☐	☐	☐

	INCLUDED IN THE SALE	EXCLUDED FROM THE SALE	NONE AT THE PROPERTY
Storage Units in Kitchen			
Kitchen Fitments:			
Fitted Cupboards and Shelves	☐	☐	☐
Refrigerator/ fridge-Freezer	☐	☐	☐
Oven	☐	☐	☐
Extractor Hood	☐	☐	☐
Hob	☐	☐	☐
Cutlery Rack	☐	☐	☐
Spice Rack	☐	☐	☐
Other (state which)			
1	☐	☐	☐
2	☐	☐	☐
3	☐	☐	☐
Kitchen Furniture:			
Washing Machine	☐	☐	☐
Dishwasher	☐	☐	☐
Tumble-Drier	☐	☐	☐
Cooker	☐	☐	☐
Other (state which)			
1	☐	☐	☐
2	☐	☐	☐
3	☐	☐	☐

	INCLUDED IN THE SALE	EXCLUDED FROM THE SALE	NONE AT THE PROPERTY
Bathroom Fitments:			
Cabinet	☐	☐	☐
Towel Rails	☐	☐	☐
Soap and Tooth-brush Holders	☐	☐	☐
Toilet Roll Holders	☐	☐	☐
Fitted Shelves/Cupboards	☐	☐	☐
Other Sanitary Fittings	☐	☐	☐
Shower			
Shower Fittings			
Shower Curtain			
Bedroom Fittings:			
Shelves	☐	☐	☐
Fitted Wardrobes	☐	☐	☐
Fitted Cupboards			
Fitted Shelving/Cupboards			
Fitted Units			
Wall Mirrors			
Picture Hooks			
Plant Holders			
Clothes Line			
Rotary Line			
Garden Shed			
Greenhouse			
Garden Ornaments			

	INCLUDED IN THE SALE	EXCLUDED FROM THE SALE	NONE AT THE PROPERTY
Trees, Plants and Shrubs			
Garden Produce			
Stock of Oil/Solid Fuel/Propane Gas			
Water Butts			
Dustbins			
Other			

Please tick the right answer

1. If you have sold through an estate agent, are all items listed in its particulars included in the sale?

YES	NO

If "NO" you should instruct the estate agent to write to everyone concerned correcting this error.

2. Do you own outright everything included in the sale?

YES	NO: (PLEASE GIVE DETAILS)

(You must give details of anything which may not be yours to sell, for example, anything rented or on HP)

_____

_____

3. (a) Have you agreed a seperate price with the buyer for any of the above items?

YES:	NO

3. (b) If "Yes" please give details of the items and the price agreed

(The price agreed must be a just and reasonable value for the items. To agree a figure which is not a just and reasonable valuation for the purposes of saving Stamp Duty Land Tax is a criminal offence. If in doubt about the correct amount you should consult a valuer).

_____

_____

_____

_____

_____

_____

NB: If you are removing any fixtures or fittings you must make good any damage caused.

You are also responsible for removing all your possessions, including rubbish, from the property, the garage, the garden, and any outbuildings or sheds.

Signed Seller(s) . . . .

. . . .

The Law Society

Information in the seller's possession or knowledge

1 ‖ Boundaries

"Boundaries" means any fence, wall, hedge or ditch which marks the edge of your property.

1.1 Looking towards the house from the road, who either owns or accepts responsibility for the boundary:

Please mark the appropriate box.

(a) on the left?

WE DO	NEXT DOOR	SHARED	NOT KNOWN

(b) on the right?

WE DO	NEXT DOOR	SHARED	NOT KNOWN

(c) across the back?

WE DO	NEXT DOOR	SHARED	NOT KNOWN

1.2 If you have answered "not known", which boundaries have you actually repaired or maintained?

(Please give details)

_____

_____

_____

1.3 Do you know of any boundary being moved in the last 20 years?

(Please give details)

_____

_____

_____

2 ‖ Disputes and complaints

2.1 Do you know of any disputes or anything which might lead to a dispute about this or any neighbouring property?

NO	YES: (PLEASE GIVE DETAILS)

_____

_____

_____

2.2 Have you received any complaints about anything you have, or have not, done as owners?

NO	YES: (PLEASE GIVE DETAILS)

2.3 Have you made any such complaints to any neighbour about what the neighbour has or has not done?

NO	YES: (PLEASE GIVE DETAILS)

3 | Notices

3.1 Have you either sent or received any letters or notices which affect your property or the neighbouring property in any way (for example, from or to neighbours, the council or a government department)?

NO	YES:	COPY ENCLOSED	TO FOLLOW	LOST

3.2 Have you had any negotiations or discussions with any neighbour or any local or other authority which affect the property in any way?

NO	YES: (PLEASE GIVE DETAILS)

4 | Guarantees

4.1 Are there any guarantees or insurance policies of the following types:

(a) NHBC Foundation 15 or Newbuild?

NO	YES	COPIES ENCLOSED	WITH DEEDS	LOST

(b) Damp course?

NO	YES	COPIES ENCLOSED	WITH DEEDS	LOST

(c) Double glazing, roof lights, roof windows, glazed doors?

NO	YES	COPIES ENCLOSED	WITH DEEDS	LOST

(d) Electrical work?

NO	YES	COPIES ENCLOSED	WITH DEEDS	LOST

(e) Roofing?

NO	YES	COPIES ENCLOSED	WITH DEEDS	LOST

(f) Rot or infestation?

NO	YES	COPIES ENCLOSED	WITH DEEDS	LOST

(g) Central heating?

NO	YES	COPIES ENCLOSED	WITH DEEDS	LOST

(h) Anything similar (e.g. cavity wall insulation, underpinning, indemnity policy)?

NO	YES	COPIES ENCLOSED	WITH DEEDS	LOST

(i) Do you have written details of the work done to obtain any of these guarantees?

NO	YES	COPIES ENCLOSED	WITH DEEDS	LOST

4.2 Have you made or considered making claims under any of these?

NO	YES: (PLEASE GIVE DETAILS)

_____

_____

_____

4.3 Do you have a maintenance or service agreement for the central heating system?

NO	YES:	COPIES ENCLOSED	WITH DEEDS	LOST

5	Services

(This section applies to gas, electrical and water supplies, sewerage disposal and telephone cables.)

5.1 Please tick which services are connected to the property.

GAS	ELEC.	MAIN WATER	MAIN DRAINS	TEL.	CABLE T.V..	SEPTIC TANK/ CESSPIT

5.2 Please supply a copy of the latest water charge account and the sewerage account (if any).

ENCLOSED	TO FOLLOW

5.3 Is the water supply on a meter?

NO	YES

5.4 Do any drains, pipes or wires for these cross any neighbour's property?

NOT KNOWN	YES: (PLEASE GIVE DETAILS)

_____

_____

_____

5.5 Do any drains, pipes or wires leading to any neighbour's property cross your property?

NOT KNOWN	YES: (PLEASE GIVE DETAILS)

5.6 Are you aware of any agreement or arrangement about any of these services?

NOT KNOWN	YES: (PLEASE GIVE DETAILS)

6 │ Sharing with the neighbours

6.1 Are you aware of any responsibility to contribute to the cost of anything used jointly, such as the repair of a shared drive, boundary or drain?

YES: (PLEASE GIVE DETAILS)	NO

6.2 Do you contribute to the cost of repair of anything used by the neighbourhood, such as the maintenance of a private road?

YES	NO

6.3 If so, who is responsible for organising the work and collecting the contributions?

6.4 Please give details of all such sums paid or owing, and explain if they are paid on a regular basis or only as and when work is required.

6.5 Do you need to go on to any neighbouring property if you have to repair or decorate your building or maintain any of the boundaries or any of the drains, pipes or wires?

YES	NO

Please mark the appropriate box

6.6 If "Yes", have you always been able to do so without objection by the neighbours?

YES	NO:	Please give details on any objection under the answer to question 2 (disputes and complaints)

6.7 Do any of your neighbours need to come onto your land to repair or decorate their building or maintain their boundaries or any drains, pipes or wires?

YES	NO

6.8 If so, have you ever objected?

NO	YES	Please give details on any objection under the answer to question 2 (disputes and complaints)

7 | Arrangements and rights

7.1 Is access obtained to any part of the property over private land, common land or a neighbour's land?
If so, please specify.

NO	YES: (PLEASE GIVE DETAILS)

7.2 Has anyone taken steps to stop, complain about or demand payment for such access being exercised?

NO	YES

7.3 Are there any other formal or informal arrangements which you have over any of your neighbours' property?

(Examples are for access or shared use.)

NO	YES: (PLEASE GIVE DETAILS)

7.4 Are there any other formal or informal arrangements which someone else has over your property?

(Examples are for access or shared use.)

NO	YES: (PLEASE GIVE DETAILS)

SELLER'S PROPERTY INFORMATION FORM (4th edition)

Address of the Property:

_____

_____

_____

IMPORTANT NOTE TO SELLERS - PLEASE READ THIS FIRST

* **Please complete this form carefully. If you are unsure how to answer the questions, ask your solicitor before doing so.**

* **This form in due course will be sent to the buyer's solicitor and will be seen by the buyer who is entitled to rely on the information.**

* For many of the questions you need only tick the correct answer. Where necessary, please give more detailed answers on a separate sheet of paper. Then send all the replies to your solicitor. This form will be passed to the buyer's solicitor.

* The answers should be those of the person whose name is on the deeds. If there is more than one of you, you should prepare the answers together.

* It is very important that your answers are correct because the buyer is entitled to rely on them in deciding whether to go ahead. Incorrect or incomplete information given to the buyer direct through your solicitor or selling agent or even mentioned to the buyer in conversation between you, may mean that the buyer can claim compensation from you or even refuse to complete the purchase.

* If you do not know the answer to any question you must say so.

* The buyer takes the property in its present physical condition and should, if necessary, seek independent advice, e.g. instruct a surveyor. You should not give the buyer your views on the condition of the property.

* If anything changes after you fill in this questionnaire but before the sale is completed, tell your solicitor immediately. THIS IS AS IMPORTANT AS GIVING THE RIGHT ANSWERS IN THE FIRST PLACE.

* Please pass to your solicitor immediately any notices you have received which affect the property, including any notices which arrive at any time before completion of your sale.

* If you have a tenant, tell your solicitor immediately if there is any change in the arrangement but do nothing without asking your solicitor first.

* You should let your solicitor have any letters, agreements or other documents which help answer the questions. If you know of any which you are not supplying with these answers, please tell your solicitor about them.

* Please complete and return the separate Fixtures, Fittings and Contents Form. It is an important document which will form part of the contract between you and the buyer. Unless you mark clearly on it the items which you wish to remove, they will be included in the sale and you will not be able to take them with you when you move.

* You may wish to delay the completion of the Fixtures, Fittings and Contents Form until you have a prospective buyer and have agreed the price.

**Peapod Solutions Limited is an
Approved Law Society Supplier**

Peapod Solutions Ltd.

8 ‖ Occupiers

8.1 Does anyone other than you live in the property?

NO	YES

If "No" go to question 9.1.
If "Yes" please give their full names and
(if under 18) their ages.

_____

_____

_____

8.2(a)(i) Do any of them have any rights to
stay on the property without your permission?

NO	YES: (PLEASE GIVE DETAILS)

(These rights may have arisen without you
realising, e.g. if they have paid towards the cost
of buying the house, paid for improvements or
helped you make your mortgage payments)

_____

_____

_____

8.2(a)(ii) Are any of them tenants or lodgers?

NO	YES: (Please give details and a copy of any Tenancy Agreement)

_____

_____

_____

8.2(b) Have they all agreed to sign the contract
for sale agreeing to leave with you (or earlier)?

NO	YES: (PLEASE GIVE DETAILS)

_____

_____

_____

9 ‖ Changes to the property

9.1 Have any of the following taken place
to the whole or any part of the property
(including the garden) and if so, when?

(a) Building works (including loft conversions
and conservatories)

NO	YES: In the year ....

(b) Change of use

NO	YES: In the year ....

(c) Sub-division

NO	YES: In the year ....

(d) Conversion

NO	YES: In the year ....

(e) Business activities

NO	YES: In the year ....

(f) Replacement windows, roof lights, roof windows, glazed doors?

NO	YES: In the year ....

If "YES" what consents were obtained under any restrictions in your title deeds?

Note: The title deeds of some properties include clauses which are called "restrictive covenants". These may, for example, forbid the owner of the property from carrying out any building work or from using it for business purposes or from parking a caravan or boat on it unless someone else (often the builder of the house) gives consent.)

9.2 Has consent under those restrictions been obtained for anything else done at the property?

YES	NO

9.3 If any consent was needed but not obtained:

(a) Please explain why not.

(b) From whom should it have been obtained?

(Note : Improvements can affect council tax banding following a sale)

9.4 Do you know if there is an indemnity policy for the property?
(Note: If consent should have been obtained under the restrictions and there is no evidence that it was obtained or there has been some problem with the title to the property or its rights or a missing planning permission, building regulation approval or completion certificate, it is sometimes necessary to take out an indemnity policy to protect the owner of the property and the lender against a future claim).

YES	NO

10	Planning and building control

10.1 Is the property used only as a private home?

YES	NO:	(PLEASE GIVE DETAILS)

10.2 (a) Has the property been designated as a Listed Building or the area designated as a Conservation Area? If so, when did this happen?

YES	NO	IN THE YEAR	NOT KNOWN

10.2 (b) Was planning permission, building regulation approval or listed building consent obtained for each of the changes mentioned in 9?

(Please list separately and supply copies of the relevant permissions and, where appropriate, certificates of completion.)

YES	NO	COPY ENCLOSED	TO FOLLOW	LOST

10.2 (c) If any of the changes mentioned in 9.1(f) have taken place, and the work completed after 1 April 2002, please supply either a FENSA certificate or a building regulation certificate.

NO	YES	COPY ENCLOSED	TO FOLLOW	LOST

11 ‖ Expenses		

Have you ever had to pay for the use of the property?	NO	YES: (PLEASE GIVE DETAILS)

(Note: Ignore council tax, water rates, and gas, electricity, and telephone bills. Disclose anything else: examples are the clearance of cesspool or septic tank, drainage rate, rent charge.)

_____

_____

_____

(If you are selling a leasehold property, details of the lease's expenses should be included on the Seller's Leasehold Information Form and not on this form.)

_____

_____

_____

12 ‖ Mechanics of the sale		

12.1 Is this sale dependent on your buying another property?	YES	NO

12.2 If "YES", what stage have the negotiations reached?

_____

_____

_____

12.3 Do you require a mortgage?	YES	NO

12.4 If "YES", has an offer been received and/or accepted or a mortgage certificate obtained?	YES	NO

13 ‖ Deposit		

Do you have the money to pay a 10% deposit on your purchase?	YES	NO

If "NO", are you expecting to use the deposit paid by your buyer to pay the deposit on your purchase?	YES	NO

14	Moving date

Please indicate if you have any special requirement about a moving date.

YES	NO

(Note: This will not be fixed until contracts are exchanged i.e. have become binding. Until then you should only make provisional removal arrangements.)

_____

_____

_____

Signature(s) ....

....

Date ....

Part II - to be completed by the seller's solicitor

The seller's solicitor should check the seller's replies to Part I against the information in the solicitor's possession. When replying to A, B, and C below the solicitor should have checked the deeds carefully, read the file and any other relevant file the firm may have by checking the filing records and, following this, make any other reasonable and prudent investigations (see the guidance from the Law Society's Conveyancing and Land Law Committee [2003] *Gazette*. 16 October, 43).

A. Is the information provided by the seller in this form consistent with the information in your possession?

Please mark the appropriate box

YES	NO

If "NO" please specify

_____
_____
_____

B. Do you have any information in your possession to supplement the information provided by the seller?

YES	NO

If "YES" please specify.

_____
_____
_____

C. Do you know if there is an indemnity policy for the property?

YES	NO

If "YES", please supply a copy.

_____
_____
_____

Reminder to solicitor

1. The Fixtures, Fittings and Contents Form should be supplied in addition to the information above.

2. Copies of all planning permissions, building regulations consents, certificates of completion, engineer's certificates, guarantees, assignments, certificates and notices should be supplied with this form.

3. If the property is leasehold, also supply the Seller's Leasehold Information Form.

4. If the property is commonhold, also supply the Seller's Commonhold Information Form.

Seller's solicitor: ....

Date: ....

The Law Society

SELLER'S LEASEHOLD INFORMATION FORM (3rd edition)

Address of the Property:

_____

_____

_____

If you live in leasehold property, please answer the following questions. Some people live in blocks of flats, others in large houses converted into flats and others in single leasehold houses. These questions cover all types of leasehold property, but some of them may not apply to your property. In that case please answer them N/A.

The instructions set out at the front of the Seller's Property Information Form apply to this form as well. Please read them again before giving your answers to these questions.

If you are unsure how to answer any of the questions, ask your solicitor.

Part I - to be completed by the seller

Information in the seller's possession or knowledge

1	Management company

1.1 If there is a management company which is run by the tenants please supply any of the following documents which are in your possession:

Please mark the appropriate box

(a) Memorandum and articles of association of the company.

ENCLOSED	TO FOLLOW	LOST	WITH THE DEEDS	N/A

(b) Your share or membership certificate.

ENCLOSED	TO FOLLOW	LOST	WITH THE DEEDS	N/A

(c) The company's accounts for the last 3 years.

ENCLOSED	TO FOLLOW	LOST	WITH THE DEEDS	N/A

(d) Copy of any regulations made by either the landlord or the company additional to the rules contained in the lease.

ENCLOSED	TO FOLLOW	LOST	WITH THE DEEDS	N/A

(e) The names and addresses of the secretary and treasurer of the company.

_____

_____

_____

(f) Has the management company been struck off the register at Companies House?

YES	NO	NOT KNOWN

1.2 If the tenants do not run the Management Company is there a Tenants' Association?

YES	NO

If "YES" please supply the contact name and address

_____
_____
_____

2 | The Landlord

2.1 What is the name and address of your landlord?

_____
_____
_____
_____

2.2 If the landlord employs an agent to collect the rent, what is the name and address of that agent?

_____
_____
_____

2.3 Please supply a receipt from the landlord for the last rent payment.

ENCLOSED	TO FOLLOW

3 | Maintenance charges

3.1 Are you liable under your lease to pay a share of the maintenance cost of the building?

YES	NO

If "NO" go to question 4.

3.2 Do you know of any expense (e.g. redecoration of outside or communal areas not usually incurred annually) likely to show in the maintenance charge accounts within the next 3 years?

YES	NO

If "YES" please give details.

_____
_____

3.3 Have maintenance charges been demanded for each of the last 3 years?

YES	NO

3.4 If so, please supply the maintenance accounts and receipts for these.

ENCLOSED	TO FOLLOW

3.5 Do you know of any problems in the last 3 years between flat owners and the landlord or management company about maintenance charges, or the method of management?

YES	NO

If "Yes", please give details.

_____
_____
_____

Please mark the appropriate box

3.6 Have you challenged the management charge or any expense in the last 3 years?

NO	YES

If "Yes", please give details.

_____
_____
_____

3.7 Do you know if the landlord has had any problems in collecting the maintenance charges from other flat owners?

NO	YES

If "Yes", please give details.

_____
_____
_____

4 │ Notices

A notice may be in a printed form or in the form of a letter and your buyer will wish to know if anything of this sort has been received.

4.1 Have you had a notice that the landlord wants to sell the building?

NO	YES	ENCLOSED	TO FOLLOW

4.2 Have you had any other notice about the building, its use, its condition or its repair and maintenance?

NO	YES	ENCLOSED	TO FOLLOW

5 │ Consents

Are you aware of any changes in the terms of the lease or of the landlord giving any consents under the lease? (This may be in a formal document, a letter or even oral.)

NO	YES	ENCLOSED	TO FOLLOW

If not in writing, please supply details.

_____
_____
_____

6 │ Complaints

6.1 Have you received any complaints from the landlord, any other landlord, management company or any other occupier about anything you have or have not done?

YES	NO

If "Yes", please give details.

_____
_____
_____

6.2 Have you complained or had cause for complaint to or about any of them?

YES	NO

If "Yes", please give details.

_____
_____
_____

7 ‖ Buildings insurance on the property

7.1 Are you responsible under the lease for arranging the buildings insurance on the property?

YES	NO

7.2 If "Yes", please supply a copy of:

(a) the insurance policy and

COPY ENCLOSED	TO FOLLOW

(b) receipt for the last payment of the premium

COPY ENCLOSED	TO FOLLOW

7.3 If NO , please supply a copy of the insurance policy arranged by the landlord or the management company and a copy of the schedule for the current year.

COPY ENCLOSED	TO FOLLOW

8 ‖ Decoration

8.1 When was the outside of the building last decorated?

IN THE YEAR	NOT KNOWN

8.2 When were any internal, communal parts last decorated?

IN THE YEAR	NOT KNOWN

8.3 When was the inside of your property last decorated?

IN THE YEAR	NOT KNOWN

9 ‖ Alterations

9.1 Are you aware of any alterations having been made to your property since the lease was originally granted?

YES	NO	NOT KNOWN

If "Yes", please supply details.

_____
_____
_____

9.2 If "Yes", was landlord's consent obtained?

NO	NOT KNOWN	NOT REQUIRED	YES	COPIES ENCLOSED	TO FOLLOW

10 | Occupation

10.1 Are you now occupying the property as your sole or main home?

YES	NO

10.2 Have you occupied the property as your sole or main home (apart from usual holidays and business trips) :

(a) continuously throughout the last 12 months?

.	YES	NO

(b) continuously throughout the last 3 years?

YES	NO

(c) for periods totalling at least 3 years during the last 10 years?

YES	NO

11 | Enfranchisement

11.1 Have you served on the landlord or any other landlord a formal notice under the enfranchisement legislation stating your desire to buy the freehold or be granted an extended lease?

NO	YES	COPY ENCLOSED	COPY TO FOLLOW

If so, please supply a copy.

11.2 If the property is a flat in a block, are you aware of the service of any notice under the enfranchisement legislation relating to the possible collective purchase of the freehold of the block or part of it?

NO	YES	COPY ENCLOSED	COPY TO FOLLOW

11.3 Have you received any response to that notice?

NO	YES	COPY ENCLOSED	COPY TO FOLLOW

Signature(s) --

Date: --

Part II - to be completed by the seller's solicitor

The seller's solicitor should check the seller's replies to Part I against the information in the solicitor's possession. When replying to A-H below the solicitor should have checked the deeds carefully, read the file and any other relevant file the firm may have by checking the filing records and, following this, make any other reasonable and prudent investigations (see the guidance from the Law Society's Conveyancing and Land Law Committee [2003] *Gazette*. 16 October, 43).

Please mark the appropriate box

A. Is the information provided by the seller in this form consistent with the information in your possession?

YES	NO

If NO, please specify

_____
_____
_____

B. Do you have any information in your possession to supplement the information provided by the seller?

YES	NO

If "YES", please specify

_____
_____
_____

C. Please provide the name and address of the recipient of notice of assignment and charge.

_____
_____
_____

D. Do the insurers make a practice of recording the interest of the buyer's mortgagee and the buyer on the policy?

YES	NO	NOT KNOWN

E. Please supply a copy of the Fire Certificate.

ENCLOSED	TO FOLLOW	NOT APPLICABLE

F. Are all of the units in the buildings or development let on identical leases? If not, in what respect do they differ?

YES	NO	NOT KNOWN

_____
_____
_____

G. Has the landlord experienced problems with the collection of maintenance charges as they fall due? If so, please supply details.

YES	NO	NOT KNOWN

_____
_____
_____

H. Is the property part of a converted building?

NO	YES

If "YES", please supply a copy of the Planning Permission or an Established Use Certificate, or evidence of permitted use.

ENCLOSED	TO FOLLOW	NOT APPLICABLE

<u>**Reminder**</u>

Copies of any relevant documents should be supplied with this form, e.g. memorandum and articles of association of the company, share or membership certificate, management accounts for the last 3 years, copy of any regulations made either by the landlord or the company additional to the rules contained in the lease, name and address of the secretary and treasurer of the company, and copies of any notices served upon the seller under sections 18-30 the Landlord and Tenant Act 1987, the Leasehold Reform Act 1967 or the Leasehold Reform Housing and Urban Development Act 1993.

Seller's solicitor   ------------------------------------

Date: ------------------------------------

The Law Society

| Transfer of whole of registered title(s) | Land Registry | **TR1** |

If you need more room than is provided for in a panel, use continuation sheet CS and attach to this form.

1. Stamp Duty

Place "X" in the appropriate box or boxes and complete the appropriate certificate.

☐ It is certified that this instrument falls within category ☐ in the Schedule to the Stamp Duty (Exempt Instruments) Regulations 1987

☐ It is certified that the transaction effected does not form part of a larger transaction or of a series of transactions in respect of which the amount or value or the aggregate amount or value of the consideration exceeds the sum of £ ☐

☐ It is certified that this is an instrument on which stamp duty is not chargeable by virtue of the provisions of section 92 of the Finance Act 2001

2. Title Number(s) of the Property *Leave blank if not yet registered.*

3. Property

4. Date

5. Transferor *Give full names and company's registered number if any.*

6. Transferee for entry on the register *Give full name(s) and company's registered number, if any. For Scottish companies use an SC prefix and for limited liability partnerships use an OC prefix before the registered number, if any. For foreign companies give territory in which incorporated.*

Unless otherwise arranged with Land Registry headquarters, a certified copy of the Transferee's constitution (in English or Welsh) will be required if it is a body corporate but is not a company registered in England and Wales or Scotland under the Companies Acts.

7. Transferee's intended address(es) for service (including postcode) for entry on the register *You may give up to three addresses for service one of which must be a postal address but does not have to be within the UK. The other addresses can be any combination of a postal address, a box number at a UK document exchange or an electronic address.*

8. The Transferor transfers the Property to the Transferee

9. Consideration *Place "X" in the appropriate box. State clearly the currency unit if other than sterling. If none of the boxes applies, insert an appropriate memorandum in the additional provisions panel.*

☐ The Transferor has received from the Transferee for the Property the sum of *In words and figures.*

☐ *Insert other receipt as appropriate.*

☐ The transfer is not for money or anything which has a monetary value

10. The Transferor transfers with *Place "X" in the appropriate box and add any modifications.*

    ⌐   full title guarantee   ⌐   limited title guarantee

11. Declaration of trust *Where there is more than one Transferee, place "X" in the appropriate box.*

    ⌐   The Transferees are to hold the Property on trust for themselves as joint tenants

    ⌐   The Transferees are to hold the Property on trust for themselves as tenants in common in equal shares

    ⌐   The Transferees are to hold the Property *Complete as necessary.*

12. Additional provisions *Insert here any required or permitted statements, certificates or applications and any agreed covenants, declarations, etc.*

13. Execution *The Transferor must execute this transfer as a deed using the space below. If there is more than one Transferor, all must execute. Forms of execution are given in Schedule 9 to the Land Registration Rules 2003. If the transfer contains Transferee's covenants or declarations or contains an application by the Transferee (e.g. for a restriction), it must also be executed by the Transferee (all of them, if there is more than one).*

Transfer of part
of registered title(s)

Land Registry

TP1

If you need more room than is provided for in a panel, use continuation sheet CS and attach to this form.

1. Stamp Duty

Place "X" in the appropriate box or boxes and complete the appropriate certificate.

☐ It is certified that this instrument falls within category ☐ in the Schedule to the Stamp Duty (Exempt Instruments) Regulations 1987

☐ It is certified that the transaction effected does not form part of a larger transaction or of a series of transactions in respect of which the amount or value or the aggregate amount or value of the consideration exceeds the sum of £ _____

☐ It is certified that this is an instrument on which stamp duty is not chargeable by virtue of the provisions of section 92 of the Finance Act 2001

2. Title number(s) out of which the Property is transferred *Leave blank if not yet registered.*

3. Other title number(s) against which matters contained in this transfer are to be registered, if any

4. Property transferred *Insert address, including postcode, or other description of the property transferred. Any physical exclusions, e.g. mines and minerals, should be defined. Any attached plan must be signed by the transferor.*

The Property is defined: *Place "X" in the appropriate box.*

☐ on the attached plan and shown *State reference e.g. "edged red".*

☐ on the Transferor's title plan and shown *State reference e.g. "edged and numbered 1 in blue".*

5. Date

6. Transferor *Give full name(s) and company's registered number, if any.*

7. Transferee for entry on the register *Give full name(s) and company's registered number, if any. For Scottish companies use an SC prefix and for limited liability partnerships use an OC prefix before the registered number, if any. For foreign companies give territory in which incorporated.*

Unless otherwise arranged with Land Registry headquarters, a certified copy of the Transferee's constitution (in English or Welsh) will be required if it is a body corporate but is not a company registered in England and Wales or Scotland under the Companies Acts.

8. Transferee's intended address(es) for service (including postcode) for entry on the register *You may give up to three addresses for service one of which must be a postal address but does not have to be within the UK. The other addresses can be any combination of a postal address, a box number at a UK document exchange or an electronic address.*

9. The Transferor transfers the Property to the Transferee

10. Consideration *Place "X" in the appropriate box. State clearly the currency unit if other than sterling. If none of the boxes applies, insert an appropriate memorandum in the additional provisions panel.*

☐ The Transferor has received from the Transferee for the Property the sum of *In words and figures.*

☐ *Insert other receipt as appropriate.*

☐ The transfer is not for money or anything which has a monetary value

11. The Transferor transfers with *Place "X" in the appropriate box and add any modifications.*

☐ full title guarantee   ☐ limited title guarantee

12. Declaration of trust *Where there is more than one Transferee, place "X" in the appropriate box.*

☐ The Transferees are to hold the Property on trust for themselves as joint tenants

☐ The Transferees are to hold the Property on trust for themselves as tenants in common in equal shares

☐ The Transferees are to hold the Property *Complete as necessary.*

13. Additional provisions
Use this panel for:
- *definitions of terms not defined above*
- *rights granted or reserved*
- *restrictive covenants*
- *other covenants*
- *agreements and declarations*
- *other agreed provisions.*

The prescribed subheadings may be added to, amended, repositioned or omitted.

Definitions

Rights granted for the benefit of the Property

Rights reserved for the benefit of other land *The land having the benefit should be defined, if necessary by reference to a plan.*

Restrictive covenants by the Transferee *Include words of covenant.*

Restrictive covenants by the Transferor *Include words of covenant.*

14. Execution *The Transferor must execute this transfer as a deed using the space below. If there is more than one Transferor, all must execute. Forms of execution are given in Schedule 9 to the Land Registration Rules 2003. If the transfer contains Transferee's covenants or declarations or contains an application by the Transferee (e.g. for a restriction), it must also be executed by the Transferee (all of them, if there is more than one).*

Application by purchaser[a] for official search with priority of the whole of the land in a registered title or a pending first registration application

Land Registry

Land Registry _____ Office

Use one form per title.
If you need more room than is provided for in a panel, use continuation sheet CS and attach to this form.

1. Administrative area and postcode if known

2. Title number *Enter the title number of the registered estate or that allotted to the pending first registration.*

3. Payment of fee [b] *Place "X" in the appropriate box.*

⌐ The Land Registry fee of £ [_____] accompanies this application.

⌐ Debit the Credit Account mentioned in panel 4 with the appropriate fee payable under the current Land Registration Fee Order.

For official use only
Impression of fees

4. The application has been lodged by:[c]
Land Registry Key No. (if appropriate)
Name
Address/DX No.

Reference[d]
Email

Telephone No.	Fax No.

5. If the result of search is to be sent to anyone other than the applicant in panel 4, please supply the name and address of the person to whom it should be sent.

Reference[d]

6. Registered proprietor/Applicant for first registration *Enter FULL name(s) of the registered proprietor(s) of the registered estate in the above mentioned title or of the person(s) applying for first registration of the property specified in panel 10. If ther are more than two, enter the first two only.*

SURNAME/COMPANY NAME:

FORENAME(S):

SURNAME/COMPANY NAME:

FORENAME(S):

7. Search from date *For a search of a registered title enter in the box a date falling within the definition of search from date in rule 131 of the Land Registration Rules 2003.*[e] *If the date entered is not such a date the application may be rejected. In the case of a **pending first registration** search, enter the letters 'FR'.*

8. Applicant *Enter FULL name of each purchaser or lessee or chargee.*

9. Reason for application I certify that the applicant intends to: *Place "X" in the appropriate box.*

☐ **P** purchase ☐ **C** take a registered charge

☐ **L** take a lease

10. Property details *Address or short description of the property.*

11. Type of search *Place "X" in the appropriate box.*

☐ **Registered land search**
Application is made to ascertain whether any adverse entry has been made in the register or day list since the date shown in panel 7.

☐ **Pending first registration search**
Application is made to ascertain whether any adverse entry has been made in the day list since the date of the pending first registration application referred to above.

**12. Signature of applicant
or their conveyancer** **Date**

Explanatory notes

■ "Purchaser" is defined in Land Registration Rules 2003, r.131. In essence, it is a person who has entered, or intends to enter, into a disposition for valuable consideration as disponee where: (i) the disposition is a registrable disposition (see Land Registration Act 2002, s.27), or (ii) there is a person subject to a duty under the Land Registration Act 2002, s.6, to apply for registration, the application is pending and the disposition would have been a registrable disposition had the estate been registered. An official search in respect of registered land made by a person other than a "purchaser" should be made in Form OS3.

■ Cheques are payable to 'Land Registry'. If you hold a credit account but do not indicate that it should be debited, and do not enclose a cheque, the registrar may still debit your account.

■ If you hold a credit account and want the official search certificate sent to an address different from that associated with your key number, enter your key number, reference and telephone number but otherwise leave panel 4 blank. Complete panel 5 instead.

■ Enter a maximum of 25 characters including stops, strokes, punctuation etc.

■ Enter the date shown as the subsisting entries date on an official copy of the register or given as the subsisting entries date at the time of an access by remote terminal.

Practice Guide 12 'Official Searches and Outline Applications' contains further information.

© Crown copyright (ref: LR/HQ) 10/03

Application by purchaser[a] for official search with priority of part of the land in a registered title or a pending first registration application

Land Registry

OS2

Land Registry _____ Office

Use one form per title. If you need more room than is provided for in a panel, use continuation sheet CS and attach to this form.

1. Administrative area and postcode if known	

2. Title number _Enter the title number of the registered estate or that allotted to the pending first registration._

3. Payment of fee[b] _Place "X" in the appropriate box._

☐ The Land Registry fee of £ [_____] accompanies this application.

☐ Debit the Credit Account mentioned in panel 4 with the appropriate fee payable under the current Land Registration Fee Order.

For official use only
Impression of fees

4. The application has been lodged by:[c]
Land Registry Key No. (if appropriate)
Name
Address/DX No.

Reference[d]
E-mail

Telephone No.	Fax No.

5. If the result of search is to be sent to anyone other than the applicant in panel 4, please supply the name and address of the person to whom it should be sent.

Reference[d]

6. Registered proprietor/Applicant for first registration _Enter FULL name(s) of the registered proprietor of the registered estate in the above mentioned title **or** of the person(s) applying for first registration of the property specified in panel 10._

SURNAME/COMPANY NAME:

FORENAME(S):

SURNAME/COMPANY NAME:

FORENAME(S):

7. Search from date *For a search of a registered title enter in the box a date falling within the definition of search from date in rule 131 of the Land Registration Rules 2003.*[c] *If the date entered is not such a date the application may be rejected. In the case of a pending first registration search, enter the letters 'FR'.*

8. Applicant *Enter FULL name of each purchaser or lessee or chargee.*

9. Reason for application I certify that the applicant intends to: *Place "X" in the appropriate box.*

☐ | P | purchase   ☐ | C | take a registered charge

☐ | L | take a lease

10. Property details *Address or short description of the property:*

Part to be searched – complete either (a) **or** (b) below
(a) Where an estate plan has been approved:

(i)   the plot number(s) is/are

(ii)   the date of approval of the estate plan is

OR

(b) Address or short description of the property as shown   on the attached plan.

NOTE: A plan in duplicate must be supplied when (b) above is completed.[1]

11. Type of search *Place "X" in the appropriate box.*

☐ **Registered land search**
Application is made to ascertain whether any adverse entry has been made in the register or day list since the date shown in panel 7.

☐ **Pending first registration search**
Application is made to ascertain whether any adverse entry has been made in the day list since the date of the pending first registration application referred to above.

**12. Signature of applicant
or their conveyancer** _____ **Date** _____

Explanatory notes

(a) "Purchaser" is defined in Land Registration Rules 2003, r.131. In essence, it is a person who has entered, or intends to enter, into a disposition for valuable consideration as disponee where: (i) the disposition is a registrable disposition (see Land Registration Act 2002, s.27), or (ii) there is a person subject to a duty under the Land Registration Act 2002, s.6, to apply for registration, the application is pending and the disposition would have been a registrable disposition had the estate been registered.
An official search in respect of registered land made by a person other than a "purchaser" should be made in Form OS3.

(b) Cheques are payable to 'Land Registry'. If you hold a credit account but do not indicate that it should be debited, and do not enclose a cheque, the registrar may still debit your account.

(c) If you hold a credit account and want the official search certificate sent to an address different from that associated with your key number, enter your key number, reference and telephone number but otherwise leave panel 4 blank. Complete panel 5 instead.

(d) Enter a maximum of 25 characters including stops, strokes, punctuation etc.

(e) Enter the date shown as the subsisting entries date on an official copy of the register or given as the subsisting entries date at the time of an access by remote terminal.

(f) The plan should show its orientation and be drawn to a stated scale preferably not less than 1/1250 for urban areas and 1/2500 for rural areas. It should clearly show by edging or colouring the extent to be searched and show sufficient details to identify the position relative to existing physical features depicted on the Ordnance Survey map and, where appropriate, show floor level(s) with sufficient dimensions to define the extent. The plan should be a copy of the plan that will be used in the protected instrument.

Practice Guide 12 'Official Searches and Outline Applications' contains further information.

**Application for an
official search
of the index map**

Land Registry

Land Registry _____ Office

If you need more room than is provided for in a panel, use continuation sheet CS and attach to this form.

1.	**Administrative area**

2.	**Property to be searched**
	Postal number or description
	Name of road
	Name of locality
	Town
	Postcode
	Ordnance Survey map reference (if known)
	Known title number(s)

3. **Payment of fee** *Place "X" in the appropriate box.*

☐ The Land Registry fee of £ [＿＿＿＿] accompanies this application.

☐ Debit the Credit Account mentioned in panel 4 with the appropriate fee payable under the current Land Registration Fee Order.

For official use only

Impression of fees

4. **The application has been lodged by:**
Land Registry Key No. (if appropriate)
Name
Address/DX No.

Reference
E-mail

Telephone No.	Fax No.

5. If the result of search is to be sent to anyone other than the applicant in panel 4, please supply the name and address of the person to whom it should be sent.

Reference _____

6. **I apply for an official search of the index map in respect of the land referred to in panel 2 above and shown** _____ **on the attached plan.**

Any attached plan must contain sufficient details of the surrounding roads and other features to enable the land to be identified satisfactorily on the Ordnance Survey map. A plan may be unnecessary if the land can be identified by postal description.

7. **Signature of applicant** _____ **Date** _____

Explanatory notes

1. The purpose and scope of Official Searches of the Index Map are described in Practice Guide 10 'Official searches of the Index Map' obtainable from any Land Registry office. It can also be viewed online at www.landregistry.gov.uk.

2. Please send this application to the appropriate Land Registry office. This information is contained in Practice Guide 51 'Areas served by Land Registry offices'.

3. Please ensure that the appropriate fee payable under the current Land Registration Fee Order accompanies your application. If paying fees by cheque or postal order, these should be crossed and payable to "Land Registry". Where you have requested that the fee be paid by Credit Account, receipt of the certificate of result is confirmation that the appropriate fee has been debited.

First registration application

If you need more room than is provided for in a panel, use continuation sheet CS and attach to this form.

Administrative area and postcode *if known*
Address or other description of the estate to be registered

On registering a rentcharge, profit a prendre in gross, or franchise, show the address as follows:- "Rentcharge, franchise etc, over 2 The Grove, Anytown, Northshire NE2 9OO".

Extent to be registered *Place "X" in the appropriate box and complete as necessary.*

☐ The land is clearly identified on the plan to the _____
Enter nature and date of deed.

☐ The land is clearly identified on the attached plan and shown _____
Enter reference e.g. "edged red".

☐ The description in panel 2 is sufficient to enable the land to be clearly identified on the Ordnance Survey map

When registering a rentcharge, profit a prendre in gross or franchise, the land to be identified is the land affected by that estate, or to which it relates.

Application, priority and fees *A fee calculator for all types of applications can be found on Land Registry's website at www.landregistry.gov.uk/fees*

Nature of applications

in priority order   Value/premium £   Fees paid £

1. **First registration of the estate**
2.
3.
4.

TOTAL £

Fee payment method: *Place "X" in the appropriate box.*
I wish to pay the appropriate fee payable under the current Land Registration Fee Order:

☐ by cheque or postal order, amount £ _____ made payable to "Land Registry".

☐ by Direct Debit under an authorised agreement with Land Registry.

FOR OFFICIAL USE ONLY
Record of fees paid

Particulars of under/over payments

Fees debited £

Reference number

The title applied for is *Place "X" in the appropriate box.*

☐ absolute freehold   ☐ absolute leasehold   ☐ good leasehold   ☐ possessory freehold
☐ possessory leasehold

Documents lodged with this form *List the documents on Form DL. We shall assume that you request the return of these documents. But we shall only assume that you request the return of a statutory declaration, subsisting lease, subsisting charge or the latest document of title (for example, any conveyance to the applicant) if you supply a certified copy of the document. If certified copies of such documents are not supplied, we may retain the originals of such documents and they may be destroyed.*

The applicant is: *Please provide the full name of the person applying to be registered as the proprietor.*

Application lodged by:
Land Registry Key No.(if appropriate)
Name (if different from the applicant)
Address/DX No.

Reference
E-mail

Telephone No.	Fax No.

FOR OFFICIAL USE ONLY
Status codes

8.	**Where you would like us to deal with someone else** *We shall deal only with the applicant, or the person lodging the application if different, unless you place "X" against one or more of the statements below and give the necessary details.*

☐   Send title information document to the person shown below

☐   Raise any requisitions or queries with the person shown below

☐   Return original documents lodged with this form (see note in panel 6) to the person shown below
If this applies only to certain documents, please specify.

Name
Address/DX No.

Reference
E-mail

Telephone No.	Fax No.

---

9.   Address(es) for service of every owner of the estate. The address(es) will be entered in the register and used for correspondence and the service of notice. *In this and panel 10, you may give up to three addresses for service **one** of which **must** be a postal address but does not have to be within the UK. The other addresses can be any combination of a postal address, a box number at a UK document exchange or an electronic address. For a company include the company's registered number, if any. For Scottish companies, use an SC prefix, and for limited liability partnerships, use an OC prefix before the registered number if any. For foreign companies give territory in which incorporated.*

Unless otherwise arranged with Land Registry headquarters, we require a certified copy of the owner's constitution (in English or Welsh) if it is a body corporate but is not a company registered in England or Wales or Scotland under the Companies Acts.

---

10. Information in respect of a chargee or mortgagee *Do not give this information if a Land Registry MD reference is printed on the charge, unless the charge has been transferred.*

Full name and address (including postcode) for service of notices and correspondence of the person entitled to be registered as proprietor of each charge. *You may give up to three addresses for service; see panel 9 as to the details you should include.*

Unless otherwise arranged with Land Registry headquarters, we require a certified copy of the chargee's constitution (in English or Welsh) it is a body corporate but is not a company registered in England and Wales or Scotland under the Companies Acts.

---

11.   Where the applicants are joint proprietors *Place "X" in the appropriate box*

☐   The applicants are holding the property on trust for themselves as joint tenants

☐   The applicants are holding the property on trust for themselves as tenants in common in equal shares

☐   The applicants are holding the property *(complete as necessary)*

---

12. Disclosable overriding interests *Place "X" in the appropriate box.*

☐   No disclosable overriding interests affect the estate

☐   Form DI accompanies this application

Rule 28 of the Land Registration Rules 2003 sets out the disclosable overriding interests that you must tell us about. You must use Form DI to tell us about any disclosable overriding interests that affect the estate.

The registrar may enter a notice of a disclosed interest in the register of title.

13. The title is based on the title documents listed in Form DL which are all those that are in the possession or control of the applicant.

Place "X" in the appropriate box. If applicable complete the second statement; include any interests disclosed only by searches other than local land charges. Any interests disclosed by searches which do not affect the estate being registered should be certified.

  ⌐ All rights, interests and claims affecting the estate known to the applicant are disclosed in the title documents and Form DI if accompanying this application. There is no-one in adverse possession of the property or any part of it.

  ⌐ In addition to the rights, interests and claims affecting the estate disclosed in the title documents or Form DI if accompanying this application, the applicant only knows of the following:

14. *Place "X" in this box if you are NOT able to give this certificate.* ⌐

We have fully examined the applicant's title to the estate, including any appurtenant rights, or are satisfied that it has been fully examined by a conveyancer in the usual way prior to this application.

15. We have authority to lodge this application and request the registrar to complete the registration.

16. Signature of applicant
    or their conveyancer _____ **Date** _____

Note: Failure to complete the form with proper care may deprive the applicant of protection under the Land Registration Act if, as a result, a mistake is made in the register.

Application for official copies of register/plan or certificate in Form CI

Land Registry _____ Office

Use one form per title. If you need more room than is provided for in a panel, use continuation sheet CS and attach to this form.

1. **Administrative area** if known

2. **Title number** if known

3. Property
Postal number or description

Name of road

Name of locality

Town

Postcode

Ordnance Survey map reference (if known)

4. Payment of fee *Place "X" in the appropriate box.*

☐ The Land Registry fee of £ [_____] accompanies this application.

☐ Debit the Credit Account mentioned in panel 5 with the appropriate fee payable under the current Land Registration Fee Order.

For official use only
Impression of fees

5. The application has been lodged by:
Land Registry Key No. (if appropriate)
Name
Address/DX No.

Reference
E-mail

Telephone No.	Fax No.

6. If the official copies are to be sent to anyone other than the applicant in panel 5, please supply the name and address of the person to whom they should be sent.

Reference

7. Where the title number is **not** quoted in panel 2, place "X" in the appropriate box(es). As regards this property, my application relates to:

☐ freehold estate ☐ caution against first registration ☐ franchise ☐ manor

☐ leasehold estate ☐ rentcharge ☐ profit a prendre in gross

8. In case there is an application for registration pending against the title, place "X" in the appropriate box:

☐ I require an official copy back-dated to the day prior to the receipt of that application **or**

☐ I require an official copy on completion of that application

9. I apply for: *Place "X" in the appropriate box(es) and indicate how many copies are required.*

☐ ____ official copy(ies) of the **register** of the above mentioned property

☐ ____ official copy(ies) of the **title plan or caution plan** of the above mentioned property

☐ ____ a certificate in Form CI, in which case **either**:

    ☐ an estate plan has been approved and the plot number is [   ]

    or

    ☐ no estate plan has been approved and a certificate is to be issued in respect of the land shown _____ on the attached plan and copy

10. Signature of applicant _____ **Date** _____

**Cancellation of entries
relating to a
registered charge**

Land Registry

DS1

This form should be accompanied by either Form AP1 or Form DS2.
If you need more room than is provided for in a panel, use continuation sheet CS and attach to this form.

1. Title Number(s) of the Property	
2. Property	
3. Date	
4. Date of charge	
5. Lender	
6. The Lender acknowledges that the property is no longer charged as security for the payment of sums due under the charge	
7. Date of Land Registry facility letter, if any	
8. *To be executed as a deed by the lender or in accordance with the above facility letter.*	

Application to change the register

Land Registry

If you need more room than is provided for in a panel, use continuation sheet CS and attach to this form.

1. Administrative area and postcode if known

2. Title number(s)

3. If you have already made this application by **outline application**, insert reference number:

4. This application affects *Place "X" in the appropriate box.*

- [ ] the **whole** of the title(s) *Go to panel 5.*
- [ ] **part** of the title(s) *Give a brief description of the property affected.*

5. Application, priority and fees *A fee calculator for all types of applications can be found on Land Registry's website at www.landregistry.gov.uk/fees*

Nature of applications numbered   Value £   Fees paid £
in priority order
1.

           TOTAL £

Fee payment method: *Place "X" in the appropriate box.*
I wish to pay the appropriate fee payable under the current Land Registration Fee Order:

- [ ] by cheque or postal order, amount £_____ made payable to "Land Registry".
- [ ] by Direct Debit under an authorised agreement with Land Registry.

FOR OFFICIAL USE ONLY
Record of fees paid

Particulars of under/over payments

Fees debited £

Reference number

6. Documents lodged with this form *Number the documents in sequence; copies should also be numbered and listed as separate documents. Alternatively you may prefer to use Form DL. If you supply the original document and a certified copy, we shall assume that you request the return of the original; if a certified copy is not supplied, we may retain the original document and it may be destroyed.*

7. The applicant is: *Please provide the full name(s) of the person(s) applying to change the register. Where a conveyancer lodges the application, the applicant is the client, not the conveyancer.*

8. The application has been lodged by:
Land Registry Key No. (if appropriate)
Name (if different from the applicant)
Address/DX No.

Reference
Email

Telephone No.	Fax No.

FOR OFFICIAL USE ONLY
Codes
Dealing

Status

9. Where you would like us to deal with someone else *We shall deal only with the applicant, or the person lodging the application if different, unless you place "X" against one or more of the statements below and give the necessary details.*

☐ Send title information document to the person shown below

☐ Raise any requisitions or queries with the person shown below

☐ Return original documents lodged with this form (see note in panel 6) to the person shown below
If this applies only to certain documents, please specify.

Name
Address/DX No.

Reference
Email

Telephone No.	Fax No.

10. Where you would like us to notify someone else that we have completed the registration of this application *Place "X" in the box and provide the name and address of the person to whom notification should be sent.*

☐ Send notification of completion to the person shown below

Name
Address/DX No.

Reference
Email

11. Address(es) for service of the proprietor(s) of the registered estate(s). The address(es) will be entered in the register and used for correspondence and the service of notice. *Place "X" in the appropriate box(es). You may give up to three addresses for service **one** of which **must** be a postal address but does not have to be within the UK. The other addresses can be any combination of a postal address, a box number at a UK document exchange or an electronic address.*

☐ Enter the address(es) from the transfer/assent/lease

☐ Enter the address(es), including postcode, as follows:

☐ Retain the address(es) currently in the register for the title(s)

12. Disclosable overriding interests *Place "X" in the appropriate box.*

☐ This is not an application to register a registrable disposition or it is but no disclosable overriding interests affect the registered estate(s) *Section 27 of the Land Registration Act 2002 lists the registrable dispositions. Rule 57 of the Land Registration Rules 2003 sets out the disclosable overriding interests. Use Form DI to tell us about any disclosable overriding interests that affect the registered estate(s) identified in panel 2.*

☐ Form DI accompanies this application

The registrar may enter a notice of a disclosed interest in the register of title.

13. Information in respect of any new charge *Do not give this information if a Land Registry MD reference is printed on the charge, unless the charge has been transferred.*

Full name and address (including postcode) for service of notices and correspondence of the person to be registered as proprietor of each charge. *You may give up to three addresses for service **one** of which **must** be a postal address but does not have to be within the UK. The other addresses can be any combination of a postal address, a box number at a UK document exchange or an electronic address. For a company include company's registered number, if any. For Scottish companies use an SC prefix and for limited liability partnerships use an OC prefix before the registered number, if any. For foreign companies give territory in which incorporated.*

Unless otherwise arranged with Land Registry headquarters, we require a certified copy of the chargee's constitution (in English or Welsh) if it is a body corporate but is not a company registered in England and Wales or Scotland under the Companies Acts.

14. Signature of applicant or their conveyancer _____ **Date** _____

Disclosable overriding interests

Land Registry

This form should be accompanied by either Form AP1 or Form FR1.

1.	**Property**

2.	**Title number(s)**

3.	**The applicant is:** *Please provide the full name of the person applying to be registered as proprietor or to change the register.*

The application has been lodged by:
Land Registry Key No. (if appropriate)
Name (if different from the applicant)
Address/DX No.

Reference
E-mail

Telephone No.	Fax No.

FOR OFFICIAL USE ONLY
Codes
Dealing

Status

4. In the panels below, please give details of any disclosable overriding interest that affects the estate to which the application relates.

Use panel 5 to tell us about any lease that is a disclosable overriding interest.

Use panel 6 to tell us about any other disclosable overriding interest. You may use as many Forms DI as necessary.

The registrar may enter notice of a disclosed interest in the register of title.

5. Please list below all unregistered disclosable leases in date order, starting with the oldest. You may use as many Forms DI as are necessary.

Please lodge a certified copy of either the original or the counterpart of each lease disclosed.

NB: If a previously noted lease has determined, the notice of it will only be cancelled on receipt of a Form CN1.

	Description of land leased	Date of Lease	Term and commencement date
e.g.	**Flat 1, garage 3 and bin store**	**24.06.2002**	**5 years from 24.06.2002**
a.			
b.			
c.			
d.			
e.			

| 6. | **Please list below any disclosable overriding interests which you have not included in panel 5** |

| a. | *Description of interest. For example, a legal easement.* |

arising by virtue of _____

Deed or circumstances in which the interest arose.
[affects the land shown _____ on the enclosed plan].

| b. | *Description of interest. For example, a legal easement.* |

arising by virtue of _____

Deed or circumstances in which the interest arose.
[affects the land shown _____ on the enclosed plan].

| c. | *Description of interest. For example, a legal easement.* |

arising by virtue of _____

Deed or circumstances in which the interest arose.
[affects the land shown _____ on the enclosed plan].

Local Land Charges Rules 1977 Schedule 1, Form C)

**The duplicate of this form must also be completed:
a carbon copy will suffice**

For directions, notes and fees see overleaf

Insert name and address of registering authority in space below

Official Number _____
(To be completed by the registering authority)

Register of local land charges

Requisition for search and official certificate of search

Requisition for search

(A separate requisition must be made in respect of each parcel of land except as explained overleaf)

fold

An official search is required in *Part(s)* _____ *of* [1]
the register of local land charges kept by the above-named
registering authority for subsisting registrations against the land
[defined in the attached plan] [2] described below.

Description of land sufficient to enable it to be identified

Name and address to which certificate is to be sent

Signature of applicant *(or his solicitor)*

_____

Date _____

Telephone number _____

Reference _____

Enclosure
Cheque/Money Order/Postal Order/Giro

Official certificate of search

To be completed by authorised officer

It is hereby certified that the search requested above
reveals no subsisting registrations [3]

or the _____ registrations described in the Schedule
hereto [3] up to and including the date of this certificate.

Signed ....

On behalf of .... [4]

Date _____

---

1 Delete if inappropriate. Otherwise insert Part(s) in which search is required.

2 Delete if inappropriate. (A plan should be furnished in duplicate if it is desired that a copy should be returned.)

3 Delete inapplicable words. (The Parts of the Schedule should be securely attached to the certificate and the number of registrations disclosed should be inserted in the space provided. Only Parts which disclose subsisting registrations should be sent.)

4 Insert name of registering authority.

LLC1   1

Directions and notes

1. This form and the duplicate should be completed and sent by post or left at the office of the registering authority.

2. A separate requisition for search should be made in respect of each parcel of land in respect of which a search is now required except where, for the purpose of a single transaction, a certificate is required in respect of two or more parcels of land which has a common boundary or are separated by a road, railway, river, stream or canal.

3. 'Parcel of Land' means land (including a building or part of a building) which is separately occupied or separated rated or, if not occupied or rated, in separate ownership. For the purpose of this definition an owner is the person who (in his own right or as a trustee for any other person) is entitled to receive the rack rent of land, or, where the land is not let at a rack rent, would be so entitled if it were so let.

4. The certificate of the result of an official search of the register refers to any subsisting registrations, recorded against the land defined in the application for search, in the Parts of the register in respect of which the search is requested. The Parts of the register record:

Part 1   General financial charges.

Part 2   Specific financial charges.

Part 3   Planning charges.

Part 4   Miscellaneous charges.

Part 5   Fenland ways maintenance charges.

Part 6   Land compensation charges.

Part 7   New towns charges.

Part 8   Civil aviation charges.

Part 9   Opencast coal charges.

Part 10   Listed building charges.

Part 11   Light obstruction notices.

Part 12   Drainage scheme charges.

5. An office copy of any entry in the register can be obtained on written request and on payment of the prescribed fee.

Fees

Official search (including issue of official certificate of search)
in any one Part of the register £2.00
in the whole of the register £6.00 (£4.00*)

and in addition, but subject to a maximum additional fee of £6, in respect of each parcel above one, where several parcels are included in the same requisition (see notes 2 and 3 above) whether the requisition is for search in the whole or any part of the register £1.00

Office copy of any entry in the register (not including a copy or extract of any plan or document filed by the registering authority) £1.50

* where the Search is made by electronic means in accordance with Rule 16 of the Local Land Charges Rules 1977

Office copy of any plan or other document filed by the
registering authority ....   Such reasonable fee as may be fixed by the registering authority according to the time and work involved.

All fees must be prepaid

Duplicate
Form LLCI

Official Number _____
(To be completed by the registering authority)

Register of local land charges

Requisition for search and official certificate of search

Requisition for search

An official search is required in *Part(s)* _____ *of* the register of local land charges kept by the above-named registering authority for subsisting registrations against the land [defined in the attached plan] described below.

fold

Description of land sufficient to enable it to be identified

Name and address to which certificate is to be sent

Signature of applicant *(or his solicitor)*

Date

Telephone number

Reference

Enclosure
Cheque/Money Order/Postal Order/Giro

Official certificate of search

To be completed by authorised officer

It is hereby certified that the search requested above reveals no subsisting registrations

or the _____ registrations described in the Schedule hereto up to and including the date of this certificate.

Signed ....

On behalf of ....

Date

LLC1

3

STANDARD ENQUIRIES OF LOCAL AUTHORITY
(2002 Edition)
Please type or use BLOCK LETTERS

A.

To (Local Authority address):

B.

Enter address of the land/property.
UPRN:
Address 1:
Address 2:
Street:
Locality:
Town/Village:
County:
Postcode

C.

Other roadways, footways and footpaths:

D.

Note: A plan in duplicate (see note D) must be attached. This form may be returned if the land/property cannot easily be identified.

Optional Enquiries are to be answered: YES/NO
(if so, please attach Optional (Part 11) Enquiries form)

Are any additional enquiries attached? YES/NO

E.

Fees of £
 are enclosed/are to be transferred by BACS.
Signed:

Dated:

Reference:

Tel. No:

Fax No:

E-mail Contact:

F.

Please reply to:

Tel:

Fax:

DX Number:

Notes:

A. Enter name and address of Council for the area. If the property is near a local authority boundary, consider raising certain enquiries (e.g. road schemes) with the adjoining Council.

B. Enter address and description of the property. Please quote the UPRN (Unique Property Reference Number) where known.

C. Enter name and/or mark on plan any other roadways, footpaths and footways abutting the property (in addition to those entered in Box B) to which a reply to enquiry 2 and 9 is required.

D. A duplicate plan is only required for 'hard copy' (e.g. non NLIS) searches. If required, the Optional (Part 11) Enquiries form, ticked where necessary, should be attached along with the relevant fee. Additional enquiries must be attached on a separate sheet in duplicate (hard copy only) and an additional fee will be charged for any that the Council is willing to answer.

E. Details of fees can be obtained from the Council, the NLIS Hub (via chosen channel) or The Law Society

F. Enter the name and address /DX number of the person or firm lodging this form.

The Law Society

Question	Question

1. PLANNING AND BUILDING REGULATIONS

1.1   Planning and Building Regulations Decisions and Pending Applications

What applications for any of the following (if applicable) have been granted, refused or are now pending?:-

(a)   planning permissions

(b)   listed building consents

(c)   conservation area consents

(d)   certificates of lawfulness of proposed use or development

(e)   building regulation approvals

(f)   building regulation completion certificates

How can copies of any of the above be obtained?

1.2.   Planning Designations and Proposals

What designations of land use for the property or the area, and what specific proposals for the property, are contained in any current adopted or proposed development plan?

2.   ROADS

Which of the roads, footways and footpaths mentioned in boxes B and C are:-

(a) highways maintainable at public expense;

(b) subject to a current legal agreement for adoption and, if so, is the agreement supported by a bond or other financial security;

(c) to be made up at the cost of the frontagers under a current Council resolution;

(d) to be adopted without cost to the frontagers under a current Council resolution.

3.   OTHER MATTERS

Apart from matters entered on the registers of local land charges, do any of the following matters apply to the property? How can copies of relevant documents be obtained?

3.1.   Land required for Public Purposes

Inclusion of the property in a category of land required for public purposes within Schedule 13 paras 5 & 6 of the Town & Country Planning Act 1990.

3.2.   Land to be acquired for Road Works

Inclusion of the property in land to be acquired for an approved scheme of Highway construction or improvement.

3.3.   Combined Drainage Agreement

Is there in force an agreement under the Building Act for drainage of any part of . the property in combination with another building through a private sewer?
Note: The sewerage undertaker for the area should also be asked this question.

3.4.   Nearby Road Schemes

Location of any part of the property within 200 metres of:

(a) the centre line of a new trunk road or special road specified in an order, draft order or scheme notified to the Council by the appropriate Secretary of State; or

(b) the centre line of a proposed alteration or improvement to an existing road, notified to the Council by the appropriate Secretary of State, involving the construction of a subway, underpass, flyover, footbridge, elevated road or dual carriageway (whether or not within existing highway limits); or

(c) the limits of construction of a proposed alteration or improvement to an existing road, notified to the Council by the appropriate Secretary of State, involving the construction of a roundabout (other than a mini roundabout) or widening by the construction of one or more additional traffic lanes; or

(d) the limits of construction of an approved new road to be constructed by the Council or an approved alteration or improvement by the Council to an existing road involving the construction of a subway, underpass, flyover, footbridge, elevated road or dual carriageway (whether or not within existing highway limits) or the construction of one of one or more additional traffic lanes; or

(e) the centre line of the possible route of a new road under proposals published for public consultation by the Council or by the appropriate Secretary of State; or

(f) the limits of construction of a possible alteration or improvement to an existing road involving the construction of a subway, underpass, flyover, footbridge, elevated road or dual carriageway (whether or not within existing highway limits) or the construction a roundabout (other than a mini roundabout) or widening by the construction of one or more additional traffic lanes, under proposals published for public consultation by the Council or by the appropriate Secretary of State.

Note: A mini-roundabout is a roundabout having a one-way circulatory carriageway around a flush or slightly raised circular marking less than 4 metres in diameter and with or without flared approaches.

3.5.   Nearby Railway Schemes

Location of any part of the property within 200 metres of the centre line of a proposed railway, tramway, light railway or monorail.

3.6   Traffic Schemes

Approval by the Council of any of the following, not yet implement, in respect of such of the roads, footways and footpaths mentioned in Box B (and, if applicable, Box C) which abut the boundaries of the property:

(a) permanent stopping up or diversion

(b) waiting or loading restrictions

(c) one way driving

(d) prohibition of driving

(e) pedestrianisation

(f) vehicle width or weight restriction

(g) traffic calming works e.g. road humps

(h) residents parking controls

(i) minor road widening or improvement

(j) pedestrian crossings

(k) cycle tracks

(l) bridge construction

3.7.   Outstanding Notices

Current notices relating to the property under legislation relating to building works, environment, health and safety at work, housing, highways or public health, other than those falling within other paragraphs of this Question 3.

3.8.   Infringement of Building Regulations

Proceedings authorised by the Council for infringement of the Building Regulations in respect of the property.

3.9.   Notices, Orders, Directions and Proceedings under Planning Acts

Subsisting notices, orders, directions, or proceedings, or whose which the Council has decided to issue, serve, make or commence in the following categories (other than those which are shown in the Official Certificate of Search or which have been withdrawn or quashed) relating to the property:

(a) enforcement notice

(b) stop notice

(c) listed building enforcement notice

(d) breach of condition notice

(e) planning contravention notice

(f) other notice relating to breach of planning control

(g) listed building repairs notice

(h) order for compulsory acquisition of a listed building with a minimum compensation provision

(i) building preservation notice

(j) direction restricting permitted development

(k) order revoking or modifying a planning permission or discontinuing an existing planning use

(l) tree preservation order

(m) proceedings for breach of a statutory planning agreement

3.10.   Conservation Area

Creation of the area before 31st August 1974 as a Conservation Area or a subsisting resolution to designate the area as a Conservation Area.

3.11.   Compulsory Purchase

Inclusion of the property in land which is subject to an enforceable order or resolution for compulsory purchase.

3.12.   Contaminated Land

(a) Entry relating to the property in the register maintained under s.78R(1) of the Environmental Protection Act 1990,

(b) Notice relating to the property served or resolved to be served under s.78B(3).

(c) Consultation with the owner or occupier of the property having taken place, or being resolved to take place under s.78G(3) in relation to anything to be done on the property as a result of adjoining or adjacent land being contaminated land

(d) Entry in the register, or notice served or resolved to be served under s.78B(3) in relation to any adjoining or adjacent land, which has been identified as contaminated land because it is in such a condition that harm or pollution of controlled waters might be caused on the property.

3.13.   Radon Gas

Location of the property in a Radon Affected Area.

Notes:

(1) Unless otherwise indicated, matters will be disclosed only if they apply directly to the property described in Box B.

(2) "Area" means any area in which property is located.

(3) References to the Council include any predecessor Council and also any council committee, sub-committee or other body or person exercising powers delegated by the Council and their "approval" includes their decision to proceed. The replies given to certain enquiries cover knowledge and actions of both the District Council and County Council.

(4) References to the provisions of particular Acts of Parliament or Regulations include any provisions which they have replaced and also include existing or future amendments or re-enactments.

(5) The replies will be given in the belief that they are in accordance with information present available to the officers of the replying Council, but none of the Council's or their officers accept legal responsibility for an incorrect reply, except negligence. Any liability for negligence extends to any person who (whether or not the enquiries were raised on his behalf) has knowledge, personally or through an agent, of the replies before the time when he purchases takes a tenancy of, or lends money on the security of the property or (if earlier) the time when becomes contractually bound to do so.

This form must be submitted in duplicate if hard copy search submitted (e.g. non NLIS)

OPTIONAL ENQUIRIES OF LOCAL AUTHORITY
(2002 Edition)

Please type or use BLOCK LETTERS

To (Local Authorty address):

Enter address of the land/property.

UPRN:

Address 1:

Address 2:

Street:

Locality:

Town/Village:

County:

Post Code:

Fees of £

are enclosed/are to be transferred by BACS

Signed:

Dated:

Reference:

Tel no:

Fax No:

E-Mail contact

Please reply to:

DX Number:

ADDITIONAL ENQUIRIES, please tick as required:

☐   4. Road proposals by private bodies

☐   5. Public paths or byways

☐   6. Advertisements

☐   7. Completion Notices

☐   8. Park and countryside

☐   9. Pipelines

☐   10. Houses in multiple occupation

☐   11. Noise Abatement

☐   12. Urban development Areas

☐   13. Enterprise Zones

☐   14. Inner urban improvement areas

☐   15. Simplified planning zones

☐   16. Land maintenance

☐   17. Mineral consultation areas

☐   18. Hazardous substance consents

☐   19. Environmental and pollution notices

☐   20. Food safety notices

☐   21. Hedgerow notices

This form must be submitted in duplicate if hard copy search submitted (e.g. non NLIS)

For Notes see Standard Enquiries of Local Authority form.

Question

ROAD PROPOSALS BY PRIVATE BODIES

4. What proposals by others [1] have the Council approved (capable of being implemented) for any of the following, the limits of construction of which are within 200 metres of the property:-

(a) The construction of a new road, or

(b) The alteration or improvement of an existing road, involving the construction, whether or not within existing highway limits, of a subway, underpass, flyover, footbridge, elevated road, dual carriageway, the construction of a roundabout (other than mini roundabout) [2] or the widening of an existing road by the construction of one or more additional traffic lanes?

PUBLIC PATHS OR BYWAYS

5.1. Is any public path, bridleway or road used as a public path or byway which abuts on, or crosses the property shown in a definitive map or revised definitive map prepared under Part IV of the National Parks and Access to the Countryside Act 1949 or Part III of the Wildlife and Countryside Act 1981?

5.2 If so, please mark its approximate route on the attached plan [3]

ADVERTISEMENTS

Entries in the Register

6.1. Please list any entries in the Register of applications, directions and decisions relating to consent for the display of advertisements.

6.2. If there are any entries, where can that Register be inspected?

Notices, Proceedings and Orders

6.3. Except as shown in the Official Certificate of Search:

(a) has any notice been given by the Secretary of State or served in   respect of a direction or proposed direction restricting deemed consent for any class of advertisement?

(b) have the Council resolved to serve a notice requiring the display of any advertisement to be discontinued?

(c) If a discontinuance notice has been served, has it been complied with to the satisfaction of the Council?

(d) have the Council resolved to serve any other notice or proceedings relating to a contravention of the control of advertisements?

(e) have the Council resolved to make an order for the special control of advertisements for the area?

COMPLETION NOTICES

7. Which of the planning permissions in force have the Council resolved to terminate by means of a completion notice under s.94 of the Town & Country Planning Act 1990?

PARKS AND COUNTRYSIDE

Areas of Outstanding Natural Beauty

8.1. Has any order under s.87 of the National Parks and Access to the Countryside Act 1949 been made?

National Parks

8.2. Is the property within a National Park designated under s.7. of the National Parks and Access to the Countryside 1949?

PIPELINES

9. Has a map been deposited under s.35 of the Pipelines Act 1962, or Schedule 7 of the Gas Act 1986, showing a pipeline laid through, or within 100 feet (30.48 metres) or the property?

HOUSES IN MULTIPLE OCCUPATION

10. Is the property included in a registration of houses scheme (houses in multiple occupation) under s.346 of the Housing Act 1985, containing control provisions as authorised by s.347 of that Act?

Question

NOISE ABATEMENT

Noise Abatement Zone

11.1 Have the Council made, or resolved to make, any noise abatement zone order under s.63 of the Control of Pollution Act 1974 for the area?

Entries in Register

11.2 Has any entry been recorded in the Noise Level Register kept pursuant to s.64 of the Control of Pollution Act 1974?

11.3. If there is any entry, how can copies be obtained and where can that Register be inspected?

URBAN DEVELOPMENT AREAS

12.1. Is the area an urban development area designated under part XVI of the Local Government, Planning and Land Act 1980?

12.2. If so, please state the name of the urban development corporation and the address of its principal office.

ENTERPRISE ZONES

13. Is the area an enterprise zone designated under Part XVIII of the Local Government, Planning and Land Act 1980?

INNER URBAN IMPROVEMENT AREAS

14. Have the Council resolved to define the area as an improvement area under s.4 of the Inner Urban Areas Act 1978?

SIMPLIFIED PLANNING ZONES

15.1. Is the area a simplified planning zone adopted or approved pursuant to s.83 of the Town & Country Act 1990?

15.2 Have the Council approved any proposal for designating the area as a simplified planning zone

LAND MAINTENANCE NOTICES

16. Have the Council authorised the service of a maintenance notice under s.215 of the Town & Country Planning Act 1990?

MINERAL CONSULTATION AREAS

17. Is the area a mineral consultation area notified by the county planning authority under Schedule 1 para 7 of the Town & Country Planning Act 1990?

HAZARDOUS SUBSTANCE CONSENTS

18.1. Please list any entries in the Register kept pursuant to s.28 of the Planning (Hazardous Substances) Act 1990.

18.2. If there are any entries:

(a) How can copies of the entries be obtained?

(b) Where can the Register be inspected?

ENVIRONMENTAL AND POLLUTION NOTICES

19. What outstanding notices or informal notices have been issued by the Council under the Environmental Protection Act or the Control of Pollution Act?

(This enquiry does not cover notices under Part IIA if Part III of the EPA, to which enquiries 16A and 5 apply)

FOOD SAFETY NOTICES

20. What outstanding statutory notices or information notices have been issued by the Council under the Food Safety Act?

HEDGEROW NOTICES

21.1 Please list any entries in the record maintained under regulation 10 of the Hedgerows Regulations 1997.

21.2 If there are any entries:

(a) how can copies of the matters entered be obtained?

(b) Where can the record be inspected?

---

(1) This enquiry refers to proposals by bodies or companies (such as private developers) other than the Council (and where appropriate the County Council) or the Secretary of State.

(2) A mini roundabout is a roundabout having a one-way circulatory carriageway around a flush or slightly raised circular marking less than 4 metres in diameter and with or without flared approaches.

(3) A plan of the property must be supplied by the enquirer if this enquiry is to be answered.

Inland Revenue

Land Transaction Return

Peapod Solutions Ltd

For official use only

Your transaction return |

How to fill in this return

The land transaction return guidance notes, SDLT6, available from the Orderline on **0845 302 1472**, will help in completion of this return

- A unique reference number **must** be entered on the return, this is the number shown on the payslip in the 'Reference' box. Payslips, PS1/SDLT, are available from the Orderline.
- Show amounts in whole pounds only, rounded down to the nearest pound.

- Leave blank any boxes that do not apply.
- The completed return should be printed off and then signed
- Staple the sheets in the top left-hand corner.
- Do not fold the return.

If you need help with any part of this return or with anything in the guidance notes, please phone the Stamp Taxes enquiry line on **0845 603 0135**, open 8.30am to 5.00pm Monday to Friday, except Bank Holidays. Calls are charged at local rates.

Starting your return |

ABOUT THE TRANSACTION

1 Type of property

Enter code from the guidance notes

2 Description of transaction

Enter code from the guidance notes

3 Interest transferred or created

Enter code from the guidance notes

4 Effective date of transaction

5 Any restrictions, covenants or conditions affecting the value of the interest transferred or granted? Put 'X' in one box

☐ Yes ☐ No

If 'yes' please provide details

6 Date of contract or conclusion of missives

7 Is any land exchanged or part-exchanged? Put 'X' in one box

☐ Yes ☐ No

If 'yes' please complete address of location
Postcode

House or building number

Rest of address, including house name, building name or flat number

8 Is the transaction pursuant to a previous option agreement? Put 'X' in one box

☐ Yes ☐ No

SDLT 1   Page 1

No   Image Available

M

ABOUT THE TAX CALCULATION

9 **Are you claiming relief?** Put 'X' in one box

☐ Yes   ☐ No

If 'yes' please show the reason

☐ Enter code from the guidance notes

Enter the charity's registered number, if available, or the company's CIS number

[   ]

For relief claimed on part of the property only, please enter the amount remaining chargeable

£ [   ] · 00

10 **What is the total consideration in money or money's worth, including any VAT actually payable for the transaction notified?**

£ [   ] · 00

11 If the total consideration for the transaction includes VAT, please state the amount

£ [   ] · 00

12 **What form does the consideration take?** Enter the relevant codes from the guidance notes

[   ] [   ] [   ] [   ]

13 **Is this transaction linked to any other(s)?** Put 'X' in one box

☐ Yes   ☐ No

Total consideration or value in money or money's worth, including VAT paid for all of the linked transactions

£ [   ] · 00

14 Total amount of tax due for this transaction

£ [   ] · 00

15 Total amount paid or enclosed with this notification

£ [   ] · 00

Does the amount paid include payment of any penalties and any interest due? Put 'X' in one box

☐ Yes   ☐ No

ABOUT NEW LEASES   If this doesn't apply, go straight to box 26 on page 3.

16 **Type of lease**

☐ Enter code from the guidance notes

17 **Start date as specified in lease**

[   ]

18 **End date as specified in lease**

[   ]

19 **Rent-free period**
Number of months

[   ]

20 **Annual starting rent inclusive of VAT (actually) payable**

£ [   ] · 00

End date for starting rent

[   ]

Later rent known? Put 'X' in one box

☐ Yes   ☐ No

21 **What is the amount of VAT, if any?**

£ [   ] · 00

22 **Total premium payable**

£ [   ] · 00

23 **Net present value upon which tax is calculated**

£ [   ] · 00

24 Total amount of tax due - premium

£ [   ] · 00

25 Total amount of tax due - NPV

£ [   ] · 00

Check the guidance notes to see if you will need to complete supplementary return 'Additional details about the transaction, including leases', SDLT4.

SDLT 1   Page 2

No   Image Available

[M   ]

ABOUT THE LAND including buildings

Where more than one piece of land is being sold or you cannot complete the address field in the space provided, please complete the supplementary return 'Additional details about the land', SDLT3.

26 Number of properties included

27 Where more than one property is involved, do you want a certificate for each property? Put 'X' in one box

☐ Yes   ☐ No

28 Address or situation of land

Postcode

House or building number

Rest of address, including house name, building name or flat number

Is the rest of the address on the supplementary return 'Additional details about the land', SDLT3?
Put 'X' in one box

☐ Yes   ☐ No

ABOUT THE VENDOR including transferor, lessor

34 Number of vendors included (Note: if more than one vendor, complete boxes 45 to 48)

35 Title Enter MR, MRS, MISS, MS or other title
Note: only complete for an individual

36 Vendor (1) surname or company name

37 Vendor (1) first name(s) Note: only complete for an individual

29 Local authority number

30 Title number, if any

31 NLPG UPRN

32 If agricultural or development land, what is the area (if known)? Put 'X' in one box

☐ Hectares   ☐ Square metres

Area

33 Is a plan attached? Please note that the form reference number should be written/displayed on map. Put 'X' in one box

☐ Yes   ☐ No

38 Vendor(1) address

Postcode

House or building number

Rest of address, including house name, building name or flat number

SDLT 1   Page 3

No   Image Available

M

ABOUT THE VENDOR CONTINUED

39 Agent's name

41 Agent's DX number

40 Agent's address
Postcode

Building number

Rest of address, including building name

42 Agent's e-mail address

43 Agent's reference

44 Agent's telephone number

ADDITIONAL VENDOR

Details of other people involved (including transferor, lessor), other than vendor(1). If more than one additional vendor please complete supplementary return 'Land Transaction Return - Additional vendor/purchaser details', SDLT2.

45 Title Enter MR, MRS, MISS, MS or other title
Note: only complete for an individual

46 Vendor (2) surname or company name

47 Vendor (2) first name(s)
Note: only complete for an individual

48 Vendor (2) address

Put 'X' in this box if the same as box 38.
If not, please give address below
Postcode

House or building number

Rest of address, including house name, building name or flat number

No   Image Available

M

ABOUT THE PURCHASER including transferee, lessee

49 Number of purchasers Included (Note: if more than one purchaser is involved, complete boxes 65 to 69)

50 National Insurance number (purchaser 1), If you have one. Note:only complete for an individual

51 Title Enter MR, MRS, MISS, MS or other title
Note: only complete for an individual

52 Purchaser (1) surname or company name

53 Purchaser (1) first name(s)
Note: only complete for an individual

54 Purchaser (1) address

Put 'X' in this box if the same address as box 28.

If not, please give address below

Postcode

House or building number

Rest of address, including house name, building name or flat number

55 Is the purchaser acting as a trustee? Put 'X' in one box

Yes   No

56 Please give a daytime telephone number - this will help us if we need to contact you about your return

57 Are the purchaser and vendor connected?
Put 'X' in one box

Yes   No

58 To which address shall we send the certificate?
Put 'X' in one box

Property (box 28)   Purchaser's (box 54)

Agent's (box 61)

59 I authorise my agent to handle correspondence on my behalf. Put 'X' in one box

Yes   No

60 Agent's name

61 Agent's address

Postcode

Building number

Rest of address, including building name

62 Agent's DX number

63 Agent's reference

64 Agent's telephone number

SDLT 1   Page 5

No   Image Available

M

ADDITIONAL PURCHASER

Details of other people involved (including transferee, lessee), other than purchaser (1). If more than one additional purchaser, please complete supplementary return 'Land Transaction Return - Additional vendor/purchaser details', SDLT2.

65 | **Title** Enter MR, MRS, MISS, MS or other title
Note: only complete for an individual

66 | **Purchaser (2) surname or company name**

67 | **Purchaser (2) first name(s)**
Note: only complete for an individual

68 | **Purchaser (2) address**

Put 'X' in this box if the same as purchaser (1) (box 54).

If not, please give address below
Postcode

House or building number

Rest of address, including house name, building name or flat number

ADDITIONAL SUPPLEMENTARY RETURNS

70 | **How many supplementary returns have you enclosed with this return?** Write the number in each box. If none, please put '0'.

Additional vendor/purchaser details, SDLT2

Additional details about the land, SDLT3

69 | **Is the purchaser acting as a trustee?** Put 'X' in one box

Yes   No

Additional details about the transaction, including leases, SDLT4

DECLARATION

71 | **The purchaser(s) must sign this return.** Read the notes in Section 1 of the guidance notes, SDLT6, 'Who should complete the Land Transaction Return?'.

If you give false information, you may face financial penalties and prosecution.
The information I have given on this return is correct and complete to the best of my knowledge and belief.

Signature of purchaser 1   Signature of purchaser 2

Please keep a copy of this return and a note of the unique reference, which is in the 'Reference' box on the payslip.

Please don't fold this return - keep it flat. Staple the sheets in the top left-hand corner.

Fill out the payslip form which the unique reference was taken and pay in accordance with the 'How to pay' instructions.

Finally, please send your completed return to:
Inland Revenue, Stamp Taxes/SDLT, Comben House, Farriers Way, NETHERTON, Merseyside, Great Britain, L30 4RN, or the DX address is: Rapid Data Capture Centre, DX725593, Bootle 9

No   Image Available

M

**Inland
Revenue**

Stamp duty land tax

Certification that no Land Transaction Return is required for a land transaction

This is a self-certificate under Section 79(3) of Finance Act 2003.

Effective date of transaction

Title number/folio number

Property or land address

Name and address of purchaser's solicitor/agent

Name(s) and address of purchaser

Name(s) and address of vendor

Please turn over

Reason no Land Transaction Return is required

✓

☐ Transfer or conveyance of a freehold interest in land (in Scotland, ownership of land or the interest of the proprietor of the *dominium util* of land) for no chargeable consideration.

☐ Transfer or assignment of a leasehold interest in land (in Scotland, assignation of a tenant's interest under a lease of land) for no chargeable consideration.

☐ Grant of lease (or in Scotland, missives of let constituting a lease) where all the following are satisfied

- the term of the lease is less than seven years, and

- the amount of any premium is not such as to attract a charge to SDLT at a rate of 1% or more (ignoring the availability of any relief), and

- the amount of any rent is not such as to attract a charge to SDLT at a rate of 1% or higher (ignoring the availability of any relief).

☐ Land transactions (other than the transfer of a freehold, assignment or grant of a lease) where the amount of the consideration is **not** such as to attract a charge to SDLT at a rate of 1% or higher (ignoring the availability of any relief).

☐ Land transactions exempt from SDLT under Schedule 3 paragraph 3 Finance Act 2003 (transactions in connection with divorce).

☐ Land transactions exempt from SDLT under Schedule 3 paragraph 4 Finance Act 2003 (variation of testamentary dispositions).

Declaration

This certificate must be signed by the person acquiring the interest. Signature by an agent is not acceptable. Where there is more than one transferee all of them must sign the certificate, except in certain circumstances (please refer to guidance notes).

I certify that for the reason given (as ticked) I do not need to submit a Land Transaction Return to the Inland Revenue.

If you give false information in this certificate you may face financial penalties and prosecution.

I declare that the information I have given in this form is true and complete to the best of my knowledge and belief.

Signature of purchaser(s)

Name (printed)

Date

COMPLETION INFORMATION AND REQUISITIONS ON TITLE (2nd EDITION)

WARNING: Replies to Requisitions 4.2 and 6.2 are treated as a solicitor's undertaking.

Property: ....

Seller: ....

Buyer: ....

1. PROPERTY INFORMATION

Has the seller notified you of any change in the written information given by and on behalf of the seller prior to exchange of contracts or have you become aware of any changes? (This includes SPIF Parts I and II, SLIF Parts I and II, Replies to Pre-Contract enquires, and correspondence between us and, if appropriate, replies to any requisitions on title already raised.)

2. VACANT POSSESSION

2.1 If vacant possession is to be given on completion:-

    (a) What arrangements will be made to hand over the keys?

    (b) By what time will the Seller have vacated the property on the completion date?

2.2 If vacant possession is not being given, please confirm that an authority to the Tenant to pay the rent to the Buyer will be handed over on completion.

3. DEEDS

3.1 If the title is unregistered, do you hold all or any of the title deeds? if not, where are they?

3.2 Please list the deeds and documents to be handed over on completion.

4. COMPLETION

4.1 Will completion take place at your office? If not, where will it take place?

4.2 If we wish to complete through the post, please confirm that:-

    (i) you undertake to adopt the Law Society's Code for Completion by Post, and

    (ii) the mortgages and charges listed in reply to 6.1 are those specified for the purpose of paragraph 3 of the Code.

5. MONEY

5.1 Please state the exact amount payable on completion. If it is not just the balance purchase money, please provide copy receipts for any rent or service charge or other payments being apportioned.

5.2   Please give:

    (a)   Name and address of your bank

_____

_____

_____

    (b)   Sort Code

_____

    (c)   Your Client Account Number to
          which monies are to be sent.

_____

6.   UNDERTAKINGS

WARNING: **A reply to this requisition is treated as an undertaking. Great care must be taken answering this requisition.**

6.1   Please list the mortgages or charges secured on the property which you undertake to redeem or discharge to the extent that they relate to the property on or before completion (this includes repayment of any discount under the Housing Acts).

6.2   Do you undertake to redeem or discharge the mortgages and charges listed in reply to 6.1 on completion and to send to us Form DS1, DS3, the receipted charges(s) or confirmation that notice of release or discharge in electronic form has been given to the Land Registry as soon as you receive them?

6.3   If you agree to adopt the current Law Society's Code for Completion by Post, please confirm that you are the duly authorised agent for the proprietor of every mortgage or charge on the property which you have undertaken, in reply to 6.2, to redeem or discharge.

....
                        Buyer's Solicitor

....
                        Seller's Solicitor

Date   ....

Date   ....

WARNING: These replies should be signed only by a person with authority to give undertakings on behalf of the firm

ADDITIONAL REQUISITIONS NOT RAISED PRIOR TO EXCHANGE

The Law Society

This form is part of The Law Society's Transaction scheme. (C) The Law Society 1994, 1998, 2004.
The Law Society is the professional body for solicitors in England and Wales

Form K16

Land Charges Act 1972

APPLICATION FOR AN OFFICIAL SEARCH
(BANKRUPTCY ONLY)

Application is hereby made for an official search in the index to the registers kept pursuant to the Land Charges Act 1972 in respect of the under-mentioned names for any subsisting entries of:

(i) petitions in bankruptcy in the register of pending actions
(ii) receiving orders in bankruptcy and bankruptcy orders in the register of writs and orders
(iii) deeds of arrangement in the register of deeds of arrangement

For Official Use Only		
#		

IMPORTANT: Please read the notes overleaf before completing the form.

NAMES TO BE SEARCHED
(Please use block letters and see Note 3 overleaf)

Forename(s)	
Surname	
Forename(s)	
Surname	
Forename(s)	
Surname	
Forename(s)	
Surname	
Forename(s)	
Surname	
Forename(s)	
Surname	

Particulars of Applicant
(see Notes 4, 5 and 6 overleaf)

KEY NUMBER   Name and address (including postcode)

Name and address (including postcode) for despatch of certificate
(Leave blank if certificate is to be returned to applicant's address)

Applicant's references:

Date

FOR OFFICIAL USE ONLY

K16   Crown Copyright ref LR/SC6A

Peapod Solutions Ltd.

SPECIAL CONDITIONS

1. (a) This contract incorporates the Standard Conditions of Sale (Fourth Edition).

   (b) The terms used in this contract have the same meaning when used in the Conditions.

2. Subject to the terms of this contract and to the Standard Conditions of Sale, the seller is to transfer the property with either full title guarantee or limited title guarantee, as specified on the front page.

3. The chattels which are on the property and are set out on any attached list are included in the sale and the buyer is to pay the chattels price for them.

4. The property is sold with vacant possession.

(or) 4. The Property is sold subject to the following leases or tenancies:

Seller's conveyancers*:

Buyer's conveyancers*:

*Adding an e-mail address authorises service by e-mail: see condition 1.3.3(b)

The Law Society

Explanatory Notes

The following notes are supplied for assistance in making the application overleaf. For further information on procedures for making applications to the Land Charges Department, see the booklet 'Computerised Land Charges Department: A practical guide for solicitors', obtainable on application to the address below.

1. **Effect of search.** The official certificate of the result of this search will have no statutory effect in relation to registered land (see Land Registration Act 1925, s.59 and Land Charges Act 1972, s.14).

2. **Fee payable.** A fee is payable for each name searched. Fees must be paid by credit account or by cheque or postal order made payable to "HM Land Registry" (see the guide referred to above).

3. **Names to be searched.** The forename(s) and surname of each individual must be entered on the appropriate lines in the relevant panel overleaf. If you are searching more than 6 names, use a second form.

4. **Key number.** If you have been allocated a key number, please take care to enter this in the space provided overleaf, whether or not you are paying fees through your credit account.

5. **Applicant's name and address.** This need not be supplied if the applicant's key number is correctly entered in the space provided overleaf.

6. **Applicant's reference.** Any reference must be limited to 10 digits, including any oblique strokes and punctuation.

7. **Despatch of this form.** When completed, send this application to the address shown below, which is printed in a position so as to fit within a standard window envelope.

⌐ THE SUPERINTENDENT   ⌐
LAND CHARGES DEPARTMENT
DX 8249 PLYMOUTH 3
PLUMER HOUSE   (see Note 7 above)
TAILYOUR ROAD
CROWNHILL
L PLYMOUTH PL6 5HY   ⌐

K16   2

CONTRACT
Incorporating the Standard Conditions of Sale (Fourth Edition)

Date   :

Seller   :

Buyer   :

Property   :
(freehold/leasehold)

Title Number/root of title   :

Specified incumbrances   :

Title guarantee   :
(full/limited)

Completion date   :

Contract rate   :

Purchase price   :

Deposit   :

Chattels price   :
(if separate)

Balance   :

The seller will sell and the buyer will buy the property for the purchase price.

WARNING	Signed
This is a formal document designed to create legal rights and legal obligations. Take advice before using it.	
	Seller/Buyer

1

www.straightforwardco.co.uk

All titles, listed below, in the Straightforward Guides Series can be purchased online, using credit card or other forms of payment by going to www.straightfowardco.co.uk A discount of 25% per title is offered with online purchases.

Law
A Straightforward Guide to:
Consumer Rights
Bankruptcy Insolvency and the Law
Employment Law
Private Tenants Rights
Family law
Small Claims in the County Court
Contract law
Intellectual Property and the law
Divorce and the law
Leaseholders Rights
The Process of Conveyancing
Knowing Your Rights and Using the Courts
Producing Your own Will
Housing Rights
The Bailiff the law and You
Probate and The Law
Company law
What to Expect When You Go to Court
Guide to Competition Law
Give me Your Money-Guide to Effective Debt Collection
Caring for a Disabled Child

General titles
Letting Property for Profit
Buying, Selling and Renting property
Buying a Home in England and France
Bookkeeping and Accounts for Small Business

Creative Writing
Freelance Writing
Writing Your own Life Story
Writing performance Poetry
Writing Romantic Fiction
Speech Writing

Teaching Your Child to Read and write
Teaching Your Child to Swim
Raising a Child-The Early Years

Creating a Successful Commercial Website
The Straightforward Business Plan
The Straightforward C.V.
Successful Public Speaking

Handling Bereavement
Play the Game-A Compendium of Rules
Individual and Personal Finance
Understanding Mental Illness
The Two Minute Message
Guide to Self Defence
Buying a Used Car
Tiling for Beginners

Go to:

www.straightforwardco.co.uk